THE ARROGANCE CYCLE

Also by Michael K. Farr

A Million Is Not Enough: How to Retire with the Money You'll Need

THE ARROGANCE CYCLE

Think You Can't Lose, Think Again

WHAT EVERY INVESTOR NEEDS TO KNOW
TO PROTECT THEIR ASSETS FROM THE NEXT BIG BUBBLE

MICHAEL K. FARR
with Edward Claflin

LYONS PRESS
Guilford, Connecticut

An imprint of Globe Pequot Press

Text design: Sheryl P. Kober
Layout artist: Mary Ballachino
Project editor: Kristen Mellitt

Library of Congress Cataloging-in-Publication Data is available on file.

ISBN 978-0-7627-6435-8

Printed in the United States of America

10 9 8 7 6 5 4 3 2 1

For Laurie, Robert, and Maggie
I love you up to the sky!

CONTENTS

Contents

FOREWORD

It's an interesting piece of writing you hold in your hands. Michael Farr starts out to write a business book, which turns into a psychology text, which becomes a tract on morals.

Read simply as a business book, *The Arrogance Cycle* will benefit businesspeople through the simple process of helping their behavior by hurting their feelings. Investment arrogance starts with the idea that we know (or know someone who knows—and, per Bernie Madoff, we should drop the acquaintance) a trick to investing that other people don't know. In a world of five billion other people, there isn't any chance of this being true. But we keep hoping for a new trick.

All arrogance cycles begin with something new—the discovery that there's a whole other side of the globe, for instance, as in the South Sea Bubble, or the discovery that you can make what's on your video screen not only be stupid but talk back, too, as in the dot-com crash. If the newness is dramatic enough, it can, like new love, make the whole world seem new. Here is something so different that it makes *everything* different. You remember how collateralized debt obligations were going to change forever the entire nature of collateral, the entire nature of debt, the entire nature— they almost succeeded with this—of obligation. But *everything* is never new. The same old rules continue to apply in the universe. Gravity abides. Howsoever epically change-making were the spice trade, the Internet, and Fannie Mae, when a treasure galleon, a computer monitor, or a tract house in Nevada is dropped from a height, it breaks.

Read as a psychology text, *The Arrogance Cycle* is even more disturbing. Your money may be mentally ill. Something in the dollar's brain chemistry causes a powerful attraction to the new.

Probably this is a useful evolutionary adaptation. What if previous generations of money had been indifferent to railroads, electricity, and automobiles? But innovation arouses strong primal drives in finance's libido, and unless these drives are channeled into healthy outlets, the result can be madness, or Lehman Brothers.

Michael Farr offers psycho-fiscal therapy. I suggest a session on his couch for your portfolio if it's exhibiting a phobia about normal investment returns or other symptoms of Arrogance Cycle Disorder.

But it is as a moral tract that *The Arrogance Cycle* achieves its real power. Pride is a sin, of course. We all know that, but none of us seems to believe it. How can pride be such a bad thing when our schools devote courses and curricula to self-esteem (even to the exclusion of reading and math, as far as I can tell from my own children's school)? We live in a society that makes frank statements like "Proud to be an American," "The Few, the Proud, the Marines"—even "Underachiever and Proud of It." We turn what would seem to be matters of fact into matters of pride: "Black Pride," "Gay Pride," "Proud to Be a Union Worker." We take pride in our homes, our jobs, our families—and, in doing so, we are the pride of our nation.

True, there's a difference between pride and arrogance. None of the phrases above would be very attractive if *arrogant* and *arrogance* were substituted for *proud* and *pride*. But it's a quantitative difference. Arrogance is pride grown large. How can something we proclaim to be a virtue become a vice by getting bigger? Is there ever too much love? Is there ever too much charity? Is there ever too much faith?

There certainly can be too much faith in your investment portfolio, if you're arrogant enough to believe your own baloney. Michael Farr gives us a sermon about why pride is still one of the seven deadly sins. Investment is a humbling business. The free market reflects the thinking of the previously mentioned five billion other people in the world. That is a vast amount of common wisdom. But the arrogant investor is too proud to listen to it. Yet, while the arrogant investor is too arrogant to be just one of the crowd, he or she also wants to be part of that crowd. Because pride needs admiration, and to be leader of the pack, you must be *in* the pack.

As one of the pack, the arrogant investor is as incapable of individual thinking as he is of listening to common wisdom. The arrogant investor is an egotist. He's paying attention to himself, and he's paying attention to how others see him. This leaves him little time and energy to pay attention where he should be paying attention—to investment.

There is a deafness and a blindness to arrogance. Pride cuts us off from others, gives us license in our hearts to abuse and exploit them. Pride is a sin in our religions because it invites us to crush people. Pride is a sin in our investments because it invites the market to crush us.

—*P. J. O'Rourke*

INTRODUCTION

It was 2007, and the sixty-six-year-old Florida investor had just put all his retirement savings into real estate.

"Why doesn't everybody buy real estate?" he asked me. "I just bought a house for $149K. I got a 3 percent three-one ARM. Sure, it's just a fixed rate for the first three years—after that, rates could go way up every year. But I don't care. I'm gonna flip it fast. It's gonna cost me $3,500 to paint, add new wall-to-wall, and plant some flowers. I'll flip it in six months for $219K! Wanna bet? Just watch me. I'm making another offer on an estate sale tomorrow before it gets listed. I know the old lady's son-in-law. He says the family just wants out. It's gonna cost me about $250K, but I'll be able to sell it for twice that in a year. What sucks is the bank is getting nervous about the loans on my house and my other two properties. But, I've gotta buy this one. I think I'll talk to one of those mortgage companies that has ads on TV. I've never tried one of those before, but I need to get some more money!"

In literature, tragedies always begin on sunny days. No thunder, ominous drumbeats, or creepy organ music. Just sunshine. The sense of well-being woos you, then overwhelms you. It draws you in and makes you feel relaxed. It's a total setup.

The cycle from hubris to humility is rife with peril and possibility. Complacency sets in. Arrogance builds, reaching a crescendo at the most dangerous moments. Then, painfully, these feelings devolve into humility, self-doubt, and even hopelessness.

Is anyone totally immune? I doubt it. All of us can fall victim to this waxing and waning between insecurity and absolute certainty: the Arrogance Cycle. Yes, anyone.

But all is not lost. Recognizing the way the psyche functions and maintaining an awareness of your own emotional bias could spell the difference between gazillion-dollar gains or a pathetic plummet.

So . . . are you dancing on diamonds? Or has the glass dance floor beneath you begun to craze and collapse?

The Arrogance Cycle will help you to recognize how it's all happened before. There are lessons to be learned from the past—from those who have gone from being perfect to being perfect asses. This book will give you a way to measure yourself and the market you're in, called the Arrogance Index. It's a new investment tool that will provide you with X-ray vision to see the lever-pulling behind the Emerald City curtain.

WHAT IS ARROGANCE?

Like porn, arrogance may cause embarrassment. We all recognize arrogance when we see it. Arrogance was epitomized by that know-it-all in your class who was always waving his or her hand at the teacher with or without the right answer. Arrogance was the supremely confident athlete (of modest ability) who sneered at lesser players and wouldn't let them on his or her team. You met arrogance in the boss who ordered you to carry out meaningless tasks without even considering the possibility that there might be another, better, way of getting things done. Arrogance is the political guru (your brother-in-law? your office mate? your neighbor?) who won't shut up, who knows what's right for the state, the nation, the world, and maybe even the universe.

In my sphere, arrogance is that sixty-six-year-old Florida investor fixated on flipping real estate. This is someone who has *seen the light*. Before he knew about the big bonanza in buying and selling houses, he lived his days in confusion and darkness. Before he saw the light, he was merely human, making the kinds of choices that other human beings make. Before he saw the light, he used to consider what proportion of his investments should go into high-risk, high-yield funds and how much he should keep in reserve in lower-risk, lower-yielding investments. Before he saw the light, he was wary of offers that promised guaranteed returns with absolute security. Before seeing the light, he worried from time to time about the big picture—the known history of boom and bust, the obvious risks of engaging in transactions (involving trillions of dollars) in derivatives markets. He used to recall the scary stories of Ponzi schemes and South Sea Bubbles and Florida land deals.

But then he saw the light, and something inside him changed. There was a profound, irreversible shift in his consciousness. It was 2007, and the world looked, to him, like a far different place than any he had known before. He recognized possibilities that had never existed previously. Limitless gains were to be had, with infinitesimal risk. He heard voices, and those voices were telling him to seize the opportunities that lay before him. The voices whispered, "Real estate—that's where the money is!"

Had these been just any voices, perhaps he would have turned a deaf ear. But no, the voices he heard were coming from some of the leaders of the financial world: men and women, educated at places like Harvard, Princeton, Yale, and Stanford, who were visionaries. They were tuned in. They told him that the world we live in now is unlike the world of five or even ten years ago—that everything is happening faster, that new products and instruments of trade are being invented even as we speak. The voices announced that the world is divided in half, with those who "get it" on one side, and those who don't on the other. They told him it was different this time!

My sixty-six-year-old Florida investor believed that finally, at last, he got it. He was, as he said, "all in." Let him *not* be numbered among the morons.

In 2007 people all around me were flipping properties like there was no tomorrow. Was I among the morons? Certainly, there were things about the investors' enthusiasm that I didn't understand. How was it possible that housing prices would keep going up? It looked to me like the housing market was in a bubble, and bubbles by their very nature will eventually explode. It wasn't clear to me who would ultimately pay the piper when the housing bubble burst. And I've never known a moment since the invention of free markets when it made sense for anyone to go "all in" with all their dough. It certainly made no sense when you were sixty-six years old and planning to live off the income from your investments.

I said as much to the Florida investor. But he did not listen. He was riding on the crest of the highest wave of the Arrogance Cycle. And when you're way up there, at that giddy height, believe me—you don't have the time or patience to listen to morons.

My View of the Cycles

Needless to say, two years later all signs of arrogance had vanished from the demeanor of the Florida investor (now sixty-eight years old) as he struggled to rebuild a portfolio from the ruins of his estate. He felt like a victim. The returns that had been promised to him never materialized. As this investor, in 2009, looked glumly at the balance remaining in his retirement account, he suffered the further indignity of reading about the escalating bonuses among CEOs who had made billions off the bubble in the real estate market. His pain was palpable. What he still failed to understand, however, was the fact that he was not a victim of banks, wheeler-dealers, geniuses, quants, or the powers that be on Wall Street. He was a victim of his own Arrogance Cycle.

Let the power of arrogance never be underestimated. It is not to be trifled with. It is an ominous and powerful force. It sneaks into the bloodstream with the first winnings in any game, and with each additional success, or promise of success, the superhuman feeling of being bulletproof emerges. It creates incentives that drive the stakes higher, lure us to play harder, and induce us to expect more than ever before. Arrogance is part of the human makeup, and as we shall see, the human mind is quite literally incapable of resisting the flood of neural signals and hormonal responses that drives arrogance ever higher.

Many other factors come into play as arrogance builds. My ego swells. Self-aggrandizement goes hand in hand with the belief that I am, in some remarkable way, exceptional. If I am exceptional, it follows that special rewards are reserved for me, and where better to realize those rewards than in my bank account? Arrogance gets reinforced by side benefits. My winnings earn me the regard of my peers. I find myself in a group of winners among winners, and their high regard begins to reinforce my own swelling ego. And soon, like the bright kid waving his hand in class and the sports superhero on the winning team, I am listening to no one but myself, hearing no voices other than the ones in my head. I am both rainmaker and the rain: omniscient, omnipotent, and omnipresent. My arrogance is complete.

Do I exaggerate? Yes, but only because exaggeration is a handy way to achieve recognition of the potential that lies in all of us. Arrogance builds in insidious ways. The early signs are difficult to detect. Over time, it will become obvious, and contagious, assuming the characteristics of mass hysteria. It takes a very calm, dispassionate ego, an exceptional sense of perspective, to look at a winning hand and say, "I am lucky . . . this once. It may never happen again"—and play your cards accordingly. It takes a rocksolid sense of personal integrity and purposefulness to deal with friends, neighbors, and relatives who are basking in sudden wealth and say to yourself, "Is this really for me?" It takes a nonconformist of the first order to question the word of the seemingly smartest kids on the block, and say "No" when they ask you to join their team. And it takes a very strong armor indeed to feel no stabs or pinpricks when others are chiding you for being behind the times, unaware, and stupendously slow to take advantage of opportunities. During the tech, dot-com bubble of the late 1990s, Warren Buffett didn't buy into the furor. He held fast to his shares of Gillette, GEICO, Coca-Cola, and the *Washington Post*, and he was ridiculed for being too old and out of it to "get it." Buffett was labeled as dotty because he refused to join the crowd.

Yes, it's hard to resist the Arrogance Cycle. But resistance is possible. It begins not with greater understanding of the market, or even the historical trends of investments; rather, it begins with your knowledge of you.

THE POWER OF INSIGHT

How *do* you behave when you have that winning hand? What are you thinking? What's your next bet?

If you can answer these questions, you'll have a much clearer view of how you could end up making decisions that will land you in trouble. In chapter 7, I provide you with an assessment tool that will help you measure your arrogance (as an investor) objectively. But for now, you can get some intuitive insight just by reflecting on how you have behaved in the past, and by looking at the various factors that influence your actions.

Do you ever "feel lucky"?

There are many definitions of "luck," and it certainly does play a role in our lives. Nearly every successful person will tell you that his or her rise in the world took a lot of hard work, yes, but almost certainly that was combined with lucky timing or lucky breaks. It's easy to recognize in retrospect that "if *this* hadn't happened" or "if I hadn't met *that* person," things would not have turned out as well as they did. Those kinds of events can be attributed to luck.

But that's not what I'm talking about here. What makes you arrogant is a *feeling* of good luck. You know the phrases: "I'm on a hot streak." "I feel like this is a winner." "I've been dealt a great hand." "My number's coming up." "The stars are aligning."

As we'll see, there are parts of your brain that are custom-designed to feed the feeling that luck is going your way. As we'll also see, that lucky feeling can send your Arrogance Index soaring—and lead to some very big mistakes.

Do you have a better knowledge of the market than others?

Education is a great thing, no question about it. I'm all for doing every bit of research you can to make yourself an educated investor. But there's a risk to watch out for: When you begin to think your research is so thorough and far-reaching that you probably know more about the subject than half the guys on Wall Street, it's a sure sign your arrogance is on the rise—perhaps even dangerously so.

Not only do folks think they've really got a market insight that others don't, but they also forget that they are competing with some of the brightest minds and most sophisticated investors in the world. Mutual fund managers with teams of analysts are plying their craft fourteen hours a day, but Fred and Ethel Average still look at lines out the door at the Apple store and figure they can "beat the street." And sometimes they can. However, there's a difference between trying to beat the street and "knowing" you can beat the street.

Do you know the right people to listen to?

We love good sources. Among friends, relatives, and financial advisors, we have our favorites when it comes to seeking advice and following their lead. After a while, we know which ones we can trust. We can observe which of them do well on their own account and which seem to have our interests at heart when they give us counsel. I'm not going to advise you to close your ears, shun your best friends, or avoid all discussion of markets and investments. That would be counterproductive, in any case, since you may be picking up a lot from them, and they may have sound ideas that you ultimately want to act upon.

What I am saying is, *be aware* of your own reactions. Our thirst for wealth, security, and a sense of well-being is inextricably linked to some very fundamental desires: to be accepted, to be respected, to be members of "the club" rather than outsiders. These are basic human drives. Deny their existence, and you can become blind to your own vulnerabilities. As we will show, with numerous examples from different societies throughout history, the desire to be accepted can easily turn into an instinct to follow the herd.

But a feeling of rightness is only a syllable away from a feeling of righteousness. And when righteousness sets in, you can be sure your arrogance is about to enter the danger zone.

Do you move quickly, and strategically, to take advantage of favorable conditions?

We don't get a shot at great opportunities every day, and when we see them, the first impulse is to take advantage immediately, before the opportunity vanishes. But all opportunities are not created equal. There are some that fit well with your overall game plan or strategy. Others do not. Does it make sense to move quickly and decisively in a direction you don't want to go?

Give yourself credit for seeing opportunities and having the ability to react to changing circumstances. But be aware that this flash of insight can make you feel arrogant. Your judgment can be easily clouded by a glitter of gold. This may indeed be the time to act, and act quickly. It may also be the exact moment when you need to determine whether you are being carried away by an idea that—even should it bear fruit—is not the best idea for *you*.

Do you have a "gut feeling" when things are going your way?

How many times have we heard the expression "Trust your gut"? How many times has trusting your gut led to a massive case of indigestion?

Consider the euphoria of watching your earnings rise with the tide of a booming market. Your heart pounds faster, excitement builds day by day as you watch your money grow. What *is* that feeling? It runs deep, deeper than any mathematical calculation. Somewhere in a primitive part of your brain, the euphoric feeling is generated and enhanced by the feeling that the world around you is becoming more secure and under your control. It's a great feeling, sure—but it can lead to pure arrogance.

WHAT THIS BOOK WILL DO FOR YOU

There are many factors that contribute to arrogance in you as an individual investor, and in society as a whole. We'll be looking at all of them.

And this is a good time to take a look. We have just been through a horrendous and alarming Arrogance Cycle, and the battlefield is strewn with the cast-off goods, the lost hopes and bright prospects of the walking wounded. Whether or not you were a direct participant in the most recent and most flagrantly destructive period of financial chaos in recent history, you certainly know others who have felt the pain and suffered the losses. Just another boom-and-bust cycle? An episode of social grief to add to a long list of bubbles that popped, leaving lives in shambles and assets in disarray? Well, yes, there are historic precedents. But this time, one factor made this most recent Arrogance Cycle more severe than most others in recent history, casting a shadow that will darken our sense of trust for many years to come.

For years, we have been living in a culture of "I Deserve It." This land of "I Deserve It" is a place where we cannot even contemplate self-denial. What we see is what we want, and we believe we should get whatever we want. The list of home comforts, luxuries, and technological goodies is endless, and the rights of ownership are assumed. I am not talking about any particular kind of greed, self-indulgence, or rampant acquisitiveness. I am talking about what happens in a society when the basic assumptions about *what I need* are inextricably mingled and confused with *what I deserve*.

Obviously, the land of "I Deserve It" is not inhabited by everyone. Millions of people in this country are barely getting by. Their basic needs are not being met. Meanwhile, "I Deserve It" has become the mantra of an ever-growing number of Americans, and when a mantra is repeated often enough, it becomes embedded in the psyche. As we will see in the next chapter, it is an attitude, a belief, an assumption that has contributed significantly to the most recent Arrogance Cycle.

In the pages ahead, we'll also look at the most blatant examples of Extreme Arrogance and Insider Arrogance. While many of the underlying factors that contribute to an Arrogance Cycle are subtle, it's relatively easy to see how extreme arrogance manifests itself, especially when there are so many examples. Take a long upswing of ever-inflating expectations on Wall Street, add the professional expectations of men and women who believe they deserve to be multimillionaires within a couple years of graduation. Remove any rules, regulations, or oversight that would inhibit the financial world's most creative minds; permit the most complex transactions to be carried out without the need for public disclosure; and you create an environment where all the elements are in place for a steady fostering of pervasive arrogance. Indeed, even after the 2008 financial collapse, it is entirely possible for arrogance to continue its rise, uninterrupted. Extreme arrogance is immune to significant reverses in the market, humiliating bankruptcies and bailouts, and even the force of public scorn. At the highest levels of "I Deserve It" culture, the supremely arrogant are just as oblivious to bad press and public reproach as they are to accepted norms of behavior. Extreme arrogance has no boundaries; therein, as we'll see, lies its remarkable allure for some individuals, and untold dangers for others.

How, then, do we protect ourselves, our investments, and our future from the highs and lows of Arrogance Cycles? As I've already suggested, part of the answer lies in our own powers of self-examination and arrogance detection. While none of us can be rescued from our innate desire to prosper along with the best of them, we *can* become more aware of how this universally shared set of expectations makes us vulnerable to our own enthusiasm. We can learn about how the Arrogance Cycle contributes to market bubbles, and how we are able to convince ourselves that we can win every time, based on very weak precedents. I will identify the three most important indicators that should warn you of a rising Arrogance Index in the stock market, and I will provide you with the self-evaluation tools that will help you clearly measure your attitude toward personal investments, and how this is likely to affect your behavior in the future.

With that awareness, I am certain, you will improve your ability to avoid the blind curves, to recognize opportunities that really exist, and to shun the promoters who exhibit the worst traits of extreme arrogance, and whose siren song is designed to seduce you into feeling impervious and untouchable as you join the herd in its perilous risk-taking behavior.

CHAPTER 1

A CLIMATE OF ARROGANCE

Are You Average?

In America, being average sucks. Scores of studies and surveys define and describe the average American, but God help you if you're him. *Average* is as close to evil as it gets in America. At least if you're below average, you're sort of unique and worthy of a little special attention. According to Wikipedia, the median age of Americans is 36.7 years, and the majority is white. The average white 36.7-year-old has an average IQ, height, weight, diet, and net worth. How would you feel if you were absolutely average according to every measure? Maybe you could claim a sort of uniqueness in the perfection of all things unremarkable.

We know that, by its definition, *average* applies to most of us. But still, we fight it. We are desperate to show that *we* have special meaning and significance. Image is critical. Image is unique. Through clothing, hairstyle, plastic surgery, type of car, size of house, lifestyle, and depth of wallet, we can prove we are special.

So, we go for anything that helps to show that we're remarkable and *above average.* As such, we believe that we *deserve* things that make us feel special. And what we believe we deserve is a lot more than we actually need. In a country where 5 percent of the world's population consumes about 25 percent of the world's supply of energy (oil, coal, and natural gas),[1] there is no bright line separating what we need (to live) from what we'd like to have (to be comfortable), and what we desire (to live in the manner to which we're accustomed, or would like to be accustomed). As "What I Need" becomes inextricably muddled with "What I Want" and "What I Deserve," the impulse to buy more—always more—goes haywire.

1

Garrison Keillor welcomes radio audiences to Lake Wobegon, "where all the women are strong, all the men are good-looking, and all the children are above average." Audiences chuckle a little uncomfortably at this a-little-too-close-to-the-truth parody of how average Americans prefer to think about their lives.

Economists and social commentators sometimes speak of "American consumerism" as if it were a given—something that is inherently part of the American psyche. Certainly, ready data support that notion. Look at 2009 spending: Among households with credit cards in the United States, the average credit card debt as of 2009 was nearly $16,000.[2] This means, on average, that we feel compelled to buy $16,000 more than what we can actually afford. Why? Where does this need, or greed, or desperate yearning for things originate, and why does it seem to be so endemic to American culture?

There are many possible answers, and pundits of all persuasions have explored most of them. Perhaps, indeed, we are a more materialistic culture. Living in a country where there was never a class of nobility, where it always seemed possible to move up and move ahead by working hard, taking advantage of opportunities, and grabbing what was available when the time was ripe, we've had, from the very beginning, the chance to cross social boundaries in ways that were largely unknown in most European cultures and, in many parts of the world, are still rare. We started out with an abundance of land and natural resources, and once the original inhabitants of North America had been conquered, there was, for the new arrivals, unbounded territory offering riches of many kinds. With industrialization came inventiveness and entrepreneurship, along with a constant influx of immigrant groups eager to achieve the ownership and affluence that would help them rise to the same level as those who had come before.

True, it would be convenient to blame American consumerism on hordes of advertising messages and phalanxes of marketing experts, but the acquisitive impulse is fundamental to human nature, and the desire for earthly goods is necessary for a sense of security. In a nation where people were constantly on the move, where families were rooted in cultures thousands of miles away, across vast oceans, the gathering of possessions was an important way to say "This is my new home." And if that accumulation was sometimes excessive, well, who was to say when enough was really enough? The trade-off between the embarrassment of *having excess* trumps the shame of *not having enough*. Accumulating enough to satisfy your needs plus having a margin for safety seems sensible— but when does *having excess* transport reasonable people to frenzied extremes that can create lasting and devastating consequences?

If a certain amount of consumerism is instinctive and inevitable, there are other, more controllable factors that account for the most egregious examples of excess. In an open society—where information flows freely, social boundaries are highly permeable, and ambitions run high—it is extremely easy to peer over your neighbor's fence and say, "I wish I had that greener grass for myself." From there, it is only a short leap of the imagination to "I *can* have that greener grass for myself." And once that is settled in the mind, nothing remains but to work for, wish for, and anticipate the opportunity to have what your neighbor has. In the movie *Wall Street* Gordon Gekko told us, "Greed is good"—and a few years later, this iconic character added (in *Wall Street: Money Never Sleeps*) that "now it seems it's legal . . . because everyone's drinking the same Kool-Aid."

Jealousy is defined as wanting what another person has. Envy is wanting what another person has and not wanting them to have it. While increasing arrogance has matched the peaks of every bubble in every market, a new everything-to-excess attitude has taken hold in the American psyche over the past three decades. Ever since the turn-down-your-thermostat austerity of the Carter administration, America has been galloping toward a state of "I

Deserve It" all of the time. Moreover, we gallop in this direction in spite of our hypocritical desire to be rich while still hating the rich.

Opportunities do come along. In the 1920s, on the rebound from the Great War, America became a land where new opportunities arose on every hand. Business boomed. This was the era when stores like Woolworth's and Montgomery Ward attracted millions of customers. The might of America was represented by the growth of industrial monsters like United States Steel, Anaconda Copper, General Electric. Shares for railroad companies like New York Central and the communications giant, American Telephone & Telegraph (AT&T), soared high.[3] The average American was allowed to own these stocks, to participate in their growth, and to revel in their triumphs. And while the stock market roared, the kings of capitalism who held great wealth and power—the Mellons, Carnegies, Rockefellers, and Harrimans—were just on the other side of the fence, where all of America could see how they lived.

In a land where there was no royalty, these tycoons were the paradigms of prosperity. Working Americans were awed by the enormous riches within view, envied (and sometimes mocked) their displays of affluence, and imagined what it would be like to live in a world where, apparently, money didn't matter. With the stock market accessible to an ever-increasing number of Americans, it began to seem as if reality could match their dreams, and the market became more than a place to make an investment and realize returns. It became a showplace where dreams of prosperity could, conceivably, be matched by real-life results. All it took, in those heady days of abundant opportunities, was a certain amount of arrogance. One needed courage to enter that market and battle it out with the titans. And as the market climbed ever higher, and millions of investors got in over their heads, arrogance was the cheapest of all commodities.

There's something simultaneously addictive and embarrassing about this sort of excess. It transports us to the world of things and not selves. It masks and ignores the noble heart and spirit that are at the core of who we are as human beings. Garrison Keillor reminds us, "Even in a time of elephantine vanity and greed, one never has to look far to see the campfires of gentle people." As the Arrogance Cycle roars, fewer gentle people may be found.

SECURITY IN POSSESSIONS

There's nothing like a stock market crash and a decade of depression to knock the wind out of an Arrogance Cycle. The collapse of the stock market in October 1929 heralded the beginning of an economic slump that took its toll on all but the most affluent. For economists, social scientists, and investors, this is one of the most-studied periods of twentieth-century economic history. Many theories have been proposed about the true causes and effects, and many conclusions have been drawn about how to avoid the replication of such a catastrophe. Was it the unfettered market—the absolute absence of meaningful regulation—that led to the crash? Or was there such optimism that a bubble was inevitable? Or, for that matter, was the stock market crash really the sole significant cause of the depression that followed?

Perhaps the crash was just one symptom of an economy that was on a collision course with disaster due to many other fundamentals related to money supply, international exchange rates, or barriers to liquidity. The debate continues and is renewed every time there is another stock market cycle of boom and bust. What is certain, however, is that the Great Depression represents one of the gloomiest specters of American history, and it could not—and would not—have happened without its accompanying Arrogance Cycle. Arrogance, that cocky assurance of guaranteed, can-do success, emboldened thousands of people to dismiss caution and discount risk. And why not? Everybody's making money; why can't I? This is my chance. I need to go for it. I need to do it.

Clearly, the 1929 stock market crash followed by the Great Depression had a profoundly dampening effect on unbridled confidence in the U.S. economic system. Optimism vanished. Shock, fear, and dread became uninvited guests in millions of households. Shock—that bank doors closed, savings vanished, jobs were lost, and homes abandoned. Fear—that there would be no food on the table, no gas in the car, no roof overhead. Dread—that the government offered no solution, that the hardscrabble years would continue interminably, that recovery was impossible.

Today, the last few survivors of that era simply shake their heads when they remember. It shaped their lives, altered their thinking. Because the causes were uncertain, the collapse sudden, the aftereffects long-lasting, the generation that experienced the Great Depression was never able to shake off the horrible presentiment that it could all happen again. Because of what they witnessed—the devastating losses, the desperation and unease of a world without a future—they did everything in their power to ensure that there wouldn't be a recurrence of the financial recklessness and the lack of oversight that seemed like the most proximate causes of the Crash. Arrogance all but vanished for a time. Who, in their right mind, could claim to be above it all? For a full decade, the United States was a land where rich bankers had been made destitute, where once-prosperous farmers could no longer feed their own families, where many of the wealthiest industrialists had been forced to declare bankruptcy, and Wall Street traders formerly brimming with confidence were rejoicing over the simple trade of a coin for an apple on a street corner. The world, truly, had been turned upside down.

My father was born in 1925 and tells stories of men coming to the door of his family's semidetached house in Washington, D.C., asking for something to eat. He proudly reports that his mother always provided a meal. It was a world that is now inconceivable to us. Can you imagine people regularly coming to your door and asking for something to eat? My grandparents raised three sons while my great-grandfather lived his last years in one of their four very small bedrooms. My grandfather was not rich. He was a clerk in a downtown jewelry store on Fifteenth Street. He worked for the same family all of his life and never had more than his salary. My grandmother was made of stern stuff and held the purse strings tightly. Frugality and living within their means navigated my family's safe financial passage through the Great Depression. Have Americans decided that this sort of economic desperation cannot happen again? Will our collective denial of risks and hard-learned lessons *prevent* it from happening again?

But even in the very midst of the Depression, a close observer would have noticed seeds being sown for the next Arrogance Cycle. In the darkened sanctuaries of movie palaces, with tickets priced to attract viewers (even nearly destitute viewers) in great numbers, the illusions of people living carefree lives became the manna of the masses. Lured with offers of two-for-one features and other incentives, some 60 to 75 million viewers flocked to movie palaces every week. In addition to gangster films like *Little Caesar, Public Enemy,* and *Scarface,* and comedies featuring Charlie Chaplin, Mae West, W. C. Fields, and the Marx Brothers, there were high-life dramas that whetted the public's taste for opulent living. MGM's *Grand Hotel* (1932) with Greta Garbo, Joan Crawford, Wallace Beery, and Lionel Barrymore set the standard for lavish settings. Fantasies like the Ginger Rogers and Fred Astaire movies (*Flying Down to Rio, The Gay Divorcee*) played alongside Busby Berkeley's over-the-top musicals, like *Roman Scandals, 42nd Street, Gold Diggers,* and *In Caliente.* Outside the movie houses there was uncertainty, stress, hunger, and doubt. Inside, Hollywood presented a fable of life as it could be lived—with women checking into fin de siècle hotels, men of unlimited wealth who dressed for dinner and ordered up whatever suited their pleasure, and visions of luxurious life in which no one would be gauche enough to mention where the next paycheck was coming from. This, then, was the view over the neighbor's fence, even though that neighbor only existed in celluloid and in the imaginations of media moguls who knew what people longed for. They were so right.

And so the cycle would begin again. In between, there would be a terrible war. (In some views, it was only the advent of World War II that put a definitive end to the Depression.) It would take the postwar investment of billions of government dollars to educate the men returning from that war, help provide them with homes, expand America's infrastructure, and, with the Marshall Plan, create the foundation of a new prosperity in Europe as well as the United States. All that lay in the future, and along with it, the inexorable rise of arrogance.

But until that happened, the Depression would cast a shadow over expectations. Humility was still part of the equation. Humility is always an essential part of the solution, but it would not last.

THE BOUNTY YEARS

Brought into a world where expectations ran high, where living standards—as they were called—were in a constant state of improvement, where unemployment was low and opportunities were many and varied, the Baby Boomers were the offspring of the postwar era. Their parents and grandparents, as it happened, were two generations trying very hard to forget. The Depression and a war were behind them. This was a new America: victorious, prosperous, and productive. Its leaders in politics, business, and industrialization had their shortcomings, but somehow they had engineered a colossal military victory and the survival of free nations. They had also raised the United States to the pinnacle of prestige and influence as a military power, an economic power, a symbol of democratic values, and a safe haven from the destructive force that had immolated swaths of the European and Asian continents.

Those Americans who had served directly in the armed forces wanted only to forget the horrors they had witnessed, the fear they had experienced, and the trials they had endured. Those who had stayed on the home front yearned to leave behind all the memories associated with that period of uncertainty and upheaval. They knew that they had earned this bounty through exceptionally hard work, lives sacrificed in battle, and tenacious American grit. Those who had escaped to America from elsewhere in the world also shared this urgent need to forget. Their goal was to leave the past, to start over, to build the future.

During the ensuing twenty-five years, there was scarcely even a recession. Gone were the images of dust-bowl shanties and breadlines, those horrific reminders of the thirties. Gone were the images of ruined cities, marching troops, skies filled with bombers, seas dotted with troopships carrying fathers, sons, and brothers to battlefields overseas. In their place was the image that we labeled the American Dream. Images of a freshly painted house, father in a suit and tie, and mother in an apron captured our imagination. The image of bright and energetic and happy kids, all busy, all smiling, all forgetting whatever they needed to forget in order to obliterate all evidence of past privations became the model. It worked pretty well. Many of those cheerful kids in their toddler outfits, the Baby Boomers, born into a world of forgetting, would not learn for many years what their parents and grandparents had endured, how America had survived its trials, and what it was like to live in a world where uncertainty and terror were the ruling forces.

It was a unique time in history. The prosperity continued, and so did the prospects of having more. And more. And more.

THE AGE OF ENTITLEMENT

Along with the arms race and the space race, Boomers have also been firsthand observers of the standard-of-living race. For a long time we were pretty sure that America was winning, and would continue to win, all three. But the standard-of-living race was the most relevant. The arms race took place in a cloud of secrecy, in missile silos under deserts and mountains, behind chain-link fences, in munitions plants and top-secret laboratories. The space race was similarly removed from day-to-day life, a series of technological miracles and missile-mounted feats that got attention during each countdown but, otherwise, was undertaken by top-level scientists who were out of sight and out of mind until each celebratory demonstration day.

As for the standard-of-living race—well, this was something else. The entire postwar generation could see it, feel it, and experience it, first year by year, then almost day by day, and finally (thanks to television), hour by hour and minute by minute. In the flush of newly won prosperity, new products were flooding the market. The most keenly desired items—cars, conveniences, stylish clothes, and rich foods—became affordable. The new home was something within reach for millions of veterans and their families.

In 1990 I was part of a congress that taught stock markets and capitalism in the Soviet Union. There were four of us: two back-office regulatory and operations guys and two front-office marketing, client-relations, and sales guys. I lectured for ten days to over 300 newly minted brokers who formed the core of this seminal renaissance of a historic communist-to-capitalist conversion. The Soviets' thirst for information was stunning. They would remain in the lecture hall as long as we would stay to talk with them. They peppered us with questions as we walked to and from our rooms. I even had to ask for a little "alone time" to use the men's room.

They were on a drive to "become New York." I countered that while they should learn from New York, they should create markets and exchanges that would be uniquely Russian. The cultural differences were vast, and I was just getting a glimpse at those differences. Most shocking was the new brokers' propensity for risk taking. At first I suspected arrogance, but I was wrong. These folks were of a generation who never had much to lose. Potential consequences meant very little to them when weighed against potential riches.

The Soviet Union fell just months after my first visit. (My mother always said that I could destroy almost anything.) As part of my role as consultant and advisor to the St. Petersburg stock exchange, I hosted two young stockbrokers in my home in Washington. I arranged sightseeing tours for them that included the U.S. Capitol and even the floor of the New York Stock Exchange. After all of that, these twenty-somethings were most awed by trips to the supermarket and shopping mall, and by the number of channels on cable. How could Americans have so much? they asked. They were sufficiently stunned that they didn't believe the life they saw was real. They suspected that it was all manufactured propaganda. As you might suspect, they wanted it all. They didn't want to return to the USSR. We actually had a tense moment when one of them wanted to skip the flight and defect. I explained my pledge to the head of the stock exchange and the irreparable damage that would be done to our countries' relationship, particularly as it involved the emergence of Russian capitalism. They reluctantly boarded their flight.

My young Russian friends had gotten a taste of the American Dream. They were intoxicated by possibility. Their horizons had been broadened, and they wanted more—much more.

What transpired, then, during twenty-five years of unprecedented distribution of benefits to middle-class America, was the winning of all three races. In the arms race, the United States built its arsenal and expanded its defenses to the point where security seemed assured. Between the Korean War and the Vietnam War was an era of minimal combat. True, the Cold War rumbled and threatened, with the fearsome specter of nuclear holocaust looming over all, but the generation that came of age in this postwar era enjoyed privileges, possessions, and, generally, a level of security unknown to their forebearers. As for the space race, after the scare of *Sputnik* and heeding the call of a young and charismatic president, America surged ahead to put the first man on the moon, a symbolic and technological triumph that swept other contenders from the field.

But it was the winning of the standard-of-living race that made the most difference to the majority of Americans. Measured by the accumulation of household conveniences and other goods, U.S. citizens held a special place in the eyes of the world. This was the flowering of the era of "I Deserve It," and for much of the middle class, the reality of economic growth and financial prosperity fed the illusion that an ever-improved standard of living would ultimately be available to all.

Reinforcing this presumption of prosperity was the level of home ownership, which increased from less than 44 percent in 1940 to 62 percent by 1960.[4] Although owning a home was a private matter, it was strongly encouraged by government incentives with the establishment of institutions like Fannie Mae and Freddie Mac, and by the generous allowance of a tax write-off for the interest on home mortgages. As prosperity spread and banks reaped the rewards of reliable income from standard loan practices in a booming economy, more credit was extended to individual consumers—first, for new "necessities" like automobiles, TVs, home appliances, and furnishings, and later, assisted by the ease of obtaining credit cards, for an ever-increasing number of luxury goods. A generation grew up in this era of expansion, contributing to the generally held assumption that our standard of living— still not fully defined, but always a form of measurement—would improve without interruption.

THE ASSUMPTIONS OF THE AFFLUENT

It would be gratifying if we could sit here today and reflect on how much the Boomer generation appreciated the enormous bounty that landed in their laps. But, as we know, this was not the case. Being given a great deal, this was a generation that felt largely entitled to what previous generations had prepared for them. Further, Boomers generally felt justified in wanting more. Several factors contributed to this mind-set, aiding and abetting a sense of entitlement.

First, as I have mentioned, there was the forgetting. The parents and grandparents of the Boomers were remarkably successful (at least at first) in erasing the memories of what had been their greatest scourges, the Depression and World War II. Certainly, the Depression was alluded to—in sentences beginning, "When I was a child. . . ." Certainly, the war was an evil cloud, and *Never again* was the refrain that referenced everything within that cloud. But the almost-conspiratorial objective of adults in postwar society was to shield their children both from the experience and from explicit details of their suffering and privation. These were embarrassing memories no one wanted to dwell on; in the postwar era, goal-focused Americans were doing everything in their power to look toward the future rather than the past.

The media became enormously powerful allies in this effort to look ahead, not behind. During wartime, the masters of advertising had learned about the extraordinary power of words, music, images, and symbols to influence the masses, and in the postwar era this knowledge of persuasive power was used for more forward-looking and creative purposes—to sell product. From cereal brands to car brands, from washing machines and watches to cigarettes and sodas, from detergents to deodorants, from toothpaste to tailored suits, products were described, displayed, heralded, praised, and flaunted as never before. Through newspapers, magazines, radio, TV, billboard signs along the highways, and famously flamboyant department-store windows, consumers were presented with a huge array of purchasable goods in what was virtually the world's greatest shopping mall. No wonder the need to acquire became so pervasive. The creation of that need was the sole objective of every consumer-product manufacturer, marketer, and advertiser throughout the nation.

In the process of forgetting the past, shopping in the present, and anticipating an even-more-prosperous future, there was, however, an unforeseen consequence. The appetite for goods, the ever-increasing need to improve the standard of living, created insatiability. For most of those growing up in this environment, it became impossible to say, "That is enough" or "This is all I need." The media were intrusive, and advertising financed this intrusion. The measurement of success in advertising was the degree to which it created and fed the restless need to, first, keep up, and then, to get ahead. What did "keeping up" mean? What was "getting ahead"? There was neither the inclination nor the necessity to answer these questions. It was all done for us. We had only to open a glossy magazine to know what "keeping up" was. We had only to turn on the TV to see what "getting ahead" was. The examples were right there, before our eyes, and the only question was how to attain these things we were meant to want.

Increasingly, the means were found. When rising wages could rise no further, there was credit, and as credit became more easily available, the barriers between *wanting* and *having* fell even lower. And, yet, among the Boomers, a strange wistfulness set in. Despite the availability of goods, the widespread extension of easy credit, there were things they couldn't have. There was still a way of life that was available only to the very, very rich. With the help of the media, it was easier than ever to look over the neighbor's fence, to see what he or she possessed. Human nature seems to make it impossible to celebrate the prosperity of others without wanting the same plethora of acquisitions for ourselves. This was the dilemma that plagued the Boomers.

WHERE ARROGANCE COMES IN

The roots of arrogance, at least in this postwar cycle, did not arise from any malevolent source, nor was it a sign of some extraordinary degree of selfishness. It was, rather, the confluence of economic and social forces combined with the extremely deft manipulation of sales and marketing tools. Goods reached consumers, but once acquired—and here was the irony—they failed to satisfy. Acquisition of greater numbers of material things simply bred more want and discontent. Expectations rose to insatiable levels. Enough was never enough.

If this is the definition of a consumer society, it is also the definition of a society that measures its very health in terms of what possessions surround us. Progress is weighed in terms of increased productivity rather than improved quality of life. Consumer confidence is assessed in terms of the willingness to go out and buy more. (Shouldn't *confidence* be measured by asking how satisfied we are with what we already have?) Even technological innovation—as it applies to the items needed for everyday living—is evaluated in terms of the ability to attract new buyers rather than the ability to provide security, contentment, or a service to society as a whole. These economic truths are self-evident, but the longer they go unquestioned, the more we are likely to see acquisition as a public good as well as a private indulgence.

Of course, I don't mean to imply that the tide of affluence carried everyone on its crest, nor that this inexorable trend of consumerism was without its critics. In the climb up the ladder of economic progress, millions could not gain a foothold. Barriers of race, geography, and chronic unemployment meant there was always an American underclass living in poverty. And there were also those who boldly and aggressively resisted the tide of consumerism, either because they were clinging to religious and cultural traditions that scorned innovation, or because they mounted a hearty resistance to the infectious enthusiasm for the next big thing. Nevertheless, expectations rose for the most part, and those expectations were followed by demand.

Today, we are living among the first, second, and third generations of the post–World War II era, and it seems fair to say that each succeeding generation has expected its baseline standard of living to be higher than the previous one's. Technological innovation has helped significantly to feed the illusion that, indeed, the lives we are living now, and the possessions within our reach, outstrip any comforts available to previous generations. Among these innovations are many of the gadgets that enhance and accelerate the very efficiency of the cycle that started it all in the first place, continually speeding production, acquisition, and innovation to ever-giddier heights. These dreamy innovations have also enhanced the consumer's desire to have the newest and coolest gizmo. Gizmos have become status symbols, and not owning them drives a sense of dissatisfaction and longing that makes the whole engine work. It's not a sense of need but "I Deserve It."

THE UNDERBELLY OF ARROGANCE

If "I Deserve It" has become the way of life—and the way of spending—for millions of Americans, there has also been an increasing divergence between those who have the purchasing power and those who don't. By 1991 the United States was lagging far behind other leading industrialized countries in terms of home ownership, household savings, and health care, while leading the world in consumer and national debt.[5] At 59 percent, home ownership in the United States lagged behind Ireland, Norway, Greece, Canada, and eight other nations. Average household debt ($71,500) was more than twice that of its nearest rivals the United Kingdom, Germany, and France (and more than six times that of an average Dutch citizen). For those outside the middle class, there were dire consequences. Compared to Canada, the United Kingdom, Switzerland,

Germany, Sweden, and Norway, by 1991 the United States had the highest poverty level (17.1 percent), the greatest number of children living below the poverty line (22.4 percent), and the highest infant mortality rate (10.4 per 1,000 live births). In number of deaths from malnutrition, the United States led France, Canada, Japan, the United Kingdom, and Norway. As the largest consumer of energy, the United States by 1991 was also, by far, the largest polluter, and it led all the European nations and Canada in crime statistics. This was the reality of the situation as America entered a period of visible affluence that would prevail throughout the decade.

Clearly, the divergence between rich and poor, the haves and have-nots, those with the ability to rack up mountains of household debt and those with insufficient food and inadequate health care, was growing wider—certainly in comparison to many other developed countries. At the same time, there was compelling evidence that the nation, as a whole, was living beyond its means. By 1991 government debt, per person, was $12,433, exceeded only by Belgium ($16,423) and Japan ($14,049). With a trade deficit in excess of $113 billion and a current account deficit of $106 billion, the United States as a nation was spending far more than it was earning.

The "I Deserve It" mentality comes at a cost, but as long as there was a virtually unlimited credit line for the individual consumer—and for the nation as a whole—payment could be deferred until some indefinite time in the future. At some point, it was said, household savings would start to grow again. Credit would tighten. The tough choices would be made. Americans would cinch in their belts and step forward to meet the challenge.

But the day of reckoning was postponed. And gone was the traditional notion of work ethic. The constitutional right to *pursue* happiness was revised to a right to *be* happy. Happiness was more than something to go after—it was something we felt we deserved. Congress wasn't even asked to vote, and a new sinister standard was born.

BRACES AND THE SCENT OF POLO

When President Jimmy Carter tried to sell the nation on new expectations, based on thriftiness and conservation, my ears perked up. He wanted us to know that such measures of restraint were not only responsible but noble. I thought, at the time, that there might be change in the air. For instance, generics started to show up on supermarket shelves. These were packaged goods in plain white boxes with bold black writing. You could get generic cake mix, toothpaste, cleanser, or cereal at slashed prices. The whole idea was to look for what you needed and base your spending on that, regardless of the advertising hype that went into the packaging. It was Carter's message packaged for consumers, and for a while it seemed as if the movement would have its followers. But the message didn't take. (Neither did generic packaging.) We quickly went from black-and-white cake mix boxes to Marni handbags, Polo cologne, and the kind of fancy silk suspenders that gentlemen call "braces."

It was the permeating scent of Polo cologne that told me a new era of arrogance was upon us. Sometime around the late eighties, you couldn't get into a car or taxi on Wall Street or K Street without smelling the stuff. It was all over the place. After that came braces. Not suspenders—braces. Because Charlie Sheen in *Wall Street* wore braces, it had become the symbol of "Greed is good," and all the true believers needed to get trousers with buttons for braces (or have the buttons sewn on by their tailors). And you had to have your hair slicked back. Indeed, the Polo cologne and the braces and the slicked-back hair said greed was not only good, it was nirvana. Austerity was for schmucks. Austerity was for the average guy. And in America, remember, no one wants to be average.

As the nineties moved in, pagers turned into cell phones, and dot-com start-ups began to emerge from basements and cubicles and garage offices. The "Greed is good" mantra became a driving force. There was no such thing as excess, because there couldn't be. If you had money, the idea was to make more of it, and when you made more, you spent more, because you were proud of what you had, albeit careless of its real worth. It would have been insane to feign restraint and frugality when that was just the opposite of what you believed in.

For instance, take my friend Bobby O. He has always been cool. He always had really cool cars and dated very pretty women (premarriage, of course). Sometime in the late eighties, Bobby showed up at a lunch with a group of friends carrying what looked like an ugly, medium-size briefcase. He put it on the lunch table, pulled out a receiver, and made a phone call! He didn't even plug it in!

I seem to recall that this very early cell phone cost something like $4,500. No, Bobby didn't really need one, but that's what made it cooler. He didn't need it, but he got one anyway. Excess was cool again.

It was about this time that I noticed a change in the general attitude toward what was attainable. I'd long treasured the words of the Declaration of Independence that proclaimed each citizen was entitled to "life, liberty, and the pursuit of happiness." *Pursuit* is the operative word. But with the dawning of the "Greed is good" era, twenty-somethings seemed to have forgotten that. What they wanted was what made them happy; this was how they understood the guarantee. And what would make them happy, they believed, was more stuff. So greed was good, stuff was theirs to be had, and happiness was what they deserved. We had arrived at the apex of arrogance. The masters of extreme arrogance (we'll look at them more closely in the next chapters) were the junk-bond dealers and the leaders of Enron and WorldCom. But clinging to the same ethos—though far below them in rank—were numerous Michael Douglas and Charlie Sheen look-alikes (and smell-alikes) with Polo cologne, buttoned braces, and slicked-back hair.

Then two things happened. The dot-com bubble burst. And there was 9/11.

A NATION GOES ARROGANT

Lost in the smoldering ash of the twin towers was America's confidence in itself as a military-industrial stronghold. The attack was as shrewd as it was devastating. Commercial passenger jets—not sophisticated military aircraft—were turned into weapons of destruction. The targets were the vital centers of the most important symbols of America's power: the soaring towers that represented its economic might, and the fortress-like Pentagon that housed its most senior military personnel. Not only was the United States attacked—for the first time since Pearl Harbor on its own soil by a foreign power—but it had been wounded by an enemy wearing robes and proclaiming jihad, by a group that practiced secrecy and stealth, using small training camps as their bases of operation. Worst of all, in the weeks, months, and years following 9/11, this enemy could not be hunted down.

D.C. was a quieter place on September 12 and in the weeks that followed. When I drove to work in the morning, I passed rows of military trucks lining Connecticut Avenue. There were camouflaged soldiers armed with machine guns on every corner of the central downtown area. My office is three blocks from the World Bank and six blocks from the White House. The military presence was intense, simultaneously calming and nerve-wracking. D.C. denizens who would normally whisk by on their way to important meetings with important people suddenly took time to greet perfect strangers and say "Good morning." Crisis had brought not only humility but kinship. We had all been attacked. We all understood the fragility of life and shared a renewed, grateful perspective.

For a nation as powerful as the United States, the sneak attack and the elusiveness of the enemy posed the ultimate frustration.

And as so often happens in such situations, where direct effective response is impossible, there was, instead, posturing. The stage was set for a level of arrogance that would make all previous Arrogance Cycles seem small by comparison.

As military preparations were made for a belligerent and decisive response to the threats of an elusive gang of terrorists, the financial giants on Wall Street and the masters of the economy in D.C. immediately set to work getting their houses back in order. The rapid recovery of Wall Street, the opening of new communication networks, and the resumption of trade on the stock exchange were nothing short of phenomenal, and it happened with a speed and efficiency that was a tribute to the men and women who engineered and carried out the turnaround. Given the circumstances, the wounding of a gigantic and complex information center at the heart of international commerce, a market collapse was inevitable. But it was less a crisis of confidence than it was the brief hospitalization of a patient who was otherwise considered hale and hearty. During the next two years, as the nation shifted onto a war footing, there was a unity of purpose that helped to overcome all signs of weakness in the market and in the economy.

In many respects, the war preparations and the ensuing on-the-ground conflicts were efficiently compartmentalized. There was, for instance, no draft, so the majority of young men and women, once they'd made the choice about whether or not to join up, could then go about their assigned roles without interfering in domestic business. It appeared that the nation, as a whole, did not need to make any significant day-to-day sacrifices to support those who were engaged in mortal combat in Iraq and Afghanistan. These were wars—at least, as they were presented to the American people—that could be undertaken and maintained for almost any length of time and at almost any cost, by a well-funded and supremely confident military establishment, which, to all appearances, was able to operate without much disruption to the rest of society. Clearly, this was a far cry from the kind of support that had been required sixty years earlier on the world's stage.

In fact, as presented to those Americans not directly engaged in the war efforts, our most important assignment as citizens was to conduct business as usual—that is, to assume a posture that would clearly show Osama bin Laden and his ilk that the country did not bear the slightest scars as the result of his attack. As it turned out, this assignment—to resume all appearances of normal life—was a role that most Americans wholeheartedly embraced. When it came to disassociating America at war from America at peace, we proved to be experts.

Meanwhile, Washington gave us a helping hand in two important ways. First of all, while granting us the illusion that we didn't have to make sacrifices for the wars (by not instituting the draft), our leaders also granted us the luxury of believing that we didn't have to pay for them, either. The estimated costs of war in Iraq and Afghanistan soared from tens of billions to several hundreds of billions—and then moved briskly along to the trillion-dollar level. After all, these were not discretionary funds that could be pruned in response to the concerns of legislators or the complaints of voters. The billions set aside for the war on terror were sacrosanct. These funds supported our troops on the ground, those who actually *were* making sacrifices. Woe betide the leader or congressperson who took a stand against supporting the troops. It was an untenable position. The alternative course, selected by those on Capitol Hill, was to convince Americans that while spending the money that *had* to be spent, no one had to bear significant consequences on the home front. (We didn't even need to raise taxes to pay for the war.)

In the classic mode of Washington decision-making, consequences were ignored. After all, time moves on, other guys take over or are elected, and then it becomes their problem. It's a fundamental characteristic of an Arrogance Cycle—the assumption that "consequences won't happen to me," even though we know that they can. Everyone in the halls of government who insisted that the money must be spent and the troops must be supported also knew that the budget wouldn't balance. But justification kicked in: Since they figured it had to be done, they also bought into the illusion that everything would work out in the long run.

(By the way, I think we're all susceptible to this kind of arrogant thinking, believing in our own bulletproof exceptionality. *I'm just a little guy. I won't get caught speeding. I won't get caught fudging my taxes. I won't get hit by lightning. After all, I've never been hit by lightning.* Before we know it, insidious rationalization begins to chip away at the grown-up part of us that knows better.)

In helping to preserve this illusion, the president and Congress were fortunate to have a willing ally in the Federal Reserve chairman, Alan Greenspan. And this was the second important way in which Washington came to the aid of all Americans in our hour of distress. With his wisdom and experience in tinkering with the economy, Greenspan fully understood the importance of easy credit—not just to the consumer, but also to the banks and financial houses that served the consumer. Perceiving that it was necessary to jump-start the economy after the blow of 9/11, Greenspan lowered interest rates eleven times between January of 2001 and the end of the year, with two more decreases by June 2003. Where the cost to the banks of borrowing money had been 6.5 percent in May of 2000, it fell to 1 percent by the middle of 2003.[6] This move had the desired effect. The markets rebounded. Evidently, we had recovered. In fact, the recovery looked so good to Greenspan that he made the executive decision to continue feeding the nation's appetite for easy credit.

The reaction of a consumer society was predictable. Money was cheap. Credit was easy. America was ready to have an orgiastic field day.

A Celebration of Spending

In the financial markets, this decision was accompanied by the suspension of the Glass-Steagall Act (more on this ahead). These and related actions would have a profound effect on the Arrogance Index among bankers, traders, and investors. But its effect on the consumer was also significant. In a very brief period of time, it served to create an environment where the stuff people wanted most was on display at fire-sale prices, and for a while it looked as if everyone could join the party.

The credit card offers poured in. Consumers with half a dozen cards or more were astonished and gratified to receive more offers in the mail—even though, in some cases, their balances were already in the tens of thousands, and they were making minimum payments. Before the holidays, low-interest or no-interest, limited-time offers arrived with a note of encouragement to spend on gifts, or take a vacation, or indulge their need for time off and relaxation. Though the names on the offers bore the imprint of familiar brands—Visa, MasterCard—their sources were sometimes puzzling. There were unheard-of banks, apparently unaffiliated with any bank the consumer had ever used before. Special-interest groups, organizations, and airlines offered cards that played up the affiliation with special designs or logos. There were gold cards, platinum cards, black cards, clear cards—each representing an opportunity and an encouragement to do precisely what the nation's leaders were urging consumers to do: enjoy the fruits of their labors and the benefits of a prosperous nation that could not be intimidated by foreign threats or domestic uncertainties. In other words, shop till you drop!

But something far better was still to come—an offer that transcended any holiday gift, grown-up toy, or vacation getaway in terms of emotional value. It was an offering that lay at the heart of the American Dream, almost too good to be true. For those who were not yet homeowners, it was the unparalleled opportunity to buy a home. For those who already owned their own home, it was a chance to scale up. For those ready to move up to mansions, now was the chance to build or buy one. For those with one mansion already, here was the chance to have two, or three, or four.

Looking back from today's vantage point, we know how it happened, and we understand the consequences. But when it was happening, even had there been full disclosure, it is unlikely that anyone with the opportunity to own a home or scale up to a bigger and better one would have passed up the chance. Why wait, when a house could be purchased with a small down payment (or none at all), by households with a small or uncertain income? What was not to like, when the house you bought this year was likely to be worth 10, 20, or 30 percent more in a couple of years' time? Where was the logic in *not* buying, when you could purchase a home that was two or three times the size of a rental property, and still pay less every month? Who could afford to miss out, when properties sold four or five years previously were now on the market at double or triple the price? Unless you were a complete contrarian, or really believed the party would soon come to an end, there was no reason not to join in.

It was the culmination of everything the American consumer had ever dreamed of, and to top it off, the influx of low-priced goods from around the world provided more bargains than we'd ever seen before. Homes with ever-increasing value could be furnished, on credit, at the lowest prices ever. Cars, games, toys, and technological by-products were all within reach, at bargain-basement prices. There was seemingly no end in sight to the stream of goods that came through the doors of this wide-open market, and we were in a mood to grab all of them.

Though many witnessed the public's insatiable appetite, few blamed the consumer, who was, after all, simply doing what he or she was supposed to do. The availability of credit, of houses and goods for sale, made it all possible. But it took no coercion whatsoever to induce consumers to take what was offered. Everyone saw something they wanted, and, for a while, it all seemed to be within reach.

The most important indicators of the Arrogance Cycle were fully on display. It was an environment where irrational exuberance flourished, where rampant speculation was rewarded with profit-taking disconnected from hard work or sacrifice, a time when every door seemed to open the way to new opportunities. As usually happens when the cycle is on the rise, money no longer meant what it was supposed to mean. Instead, it had taken on a form, shape, and substance quite foreign to its original design.

CHAPTER 2

ARROGANCE IN INVESTING

Partial Truths

Imagine you've never tried cold pomegranate juice. Up until a recent trip to Jerusalem, I hadn't. I was traveling with my friend, Dr. Jeffrey Lacker, president of the Federal Reserve Bank of Richmond, for a Global Interdependence Center conference to deliver speeches at Hebrew University.

On a stifling hot walk through the old city, there were several shops advertising ice-cold pomegranate juice. I confess that I couldn't really imagine how pomegranate juice would taste, and I didn't want to find out. Eventually, one of our group tried it and pronounced it delicious. Figuring that at least it would be wet and cold, I went for it. Yes! It was awesome. Really good. I loved pomegranate juice. It was a really hot day, so I indulged in several more glasses of the cold drink.

Don't you think that someone might have told me of its superior efficacy as a laxative? Newness and near-term relief led to excess and, ultimately, to remarkable pain.

The lesson? Changing your mind about something follows a pattern. New thoughts and ideas (and juices) require us to assess and judge, to act or not act. My only previous experience with pomegranates had been eating a few of the pulpy seeds that my grandmother gave me to try as a child. They were more seed than fruit, and very bitter-tasting. I couldn't imagine how the juice would be much better.

Elisabeth Kübler-Ross wrote a great book about the five stages of grief that are associated with death and dying (and I reflected on them at length in Israel during my post-pomegranate-juice experience). While it is a very enlightening book, I think the five steps can be simplified to three: denial, acceptance, and capitulation.

Consider a new bull market in real estate. Housing prices are going up, and you don't believe it. You think that this surge will be temporary and that prices will return to their previously lower levels. While you're waiting for them to drift lower, the damn things go even higher. After a while you begin to figure that this new level actually might last. *And* as you're thinking that the prices might be stable, they, of course, go higher, and you decide you want in.

You can't understand it, but the prices are going up, and you know a handful of morons are getting rich while you sit around, asking the reasonable questions. After not too much reflection you decide that reasonable questions have left you at profit's altar for the last time. You'll be damned if you'll ask any more of those reasonable questions that were keeping you sideline-bound, and you *will* buy! You've got to get in on some of this fabulous real estate! Never mind that prices are up 250 percent and have never before been this high.

Does this sequence of thoughts and emotions sound familiar? It's the equivalent of the grieving process. In any bear or bull market, investors go through three psychological stages as the Arrogance Index begins to ramp up. The first is denial; the second, acceptance; and the third is capitulation.

Do you remember the growing awareness of the real estate boom? For many it was the sale of a neighbor's house for a record price that first caught our attention. A year or two later, even those first startling prices seemed paltry. Do you remember when you thought the prices in your neighborhood had become silly? And do you remember how you felt when they went higher still? You couldn't explain why a three-bedroom house was worth $750,000, but when you saw that price, it was thrilling because, then, just figure what yours must be worth! You smiled to yourself, harboring some quiet doubt, but still feeling quite rich. Cool!

And there you have it: You were caught up in an Arrogance Cycle. It felt great while it lasted. Maybe you escaped unscathed, or maybe you got nailed.

As the housing bubble expanded, then exploded, this progression became indisputable. I saw folks make money and lose money, and many of their stories were tragic.

One of my friends, a successful real estate developer, had a live-in housekeeper from South America who had been with the family for twenty years. Thinking ahead to the housekeeper's retirement, my generous friend had bought her a $150,000 house and made all the payments so she would own the house outright when she no longer worked for him. After a period of time, this is just what transpired.

As her financial situation improved, she brought her kids from South America; they moved in, went to school, and got jobs. The value of the house soared to $300,000. The kids saw what was happening in the real estate market and concluded there was something smarter that Mom could do with an asset like that. They encouraged her to take out a mortgage where there had been none. Using the equity as down payments, the kids then took out teaser loans on several different properties. They figured that if there was a problem with any of the properties, they could sell, get out, and pay back the principal on their mom's house.

We know what happened. The bubble burst. All the properties were underwater, the kids couldn't get the money back, and they couldn't afford the mortgage payments on their mom's house, either. Their entire investment was lost, and their mom's house along with it.

In brief, this is a perfect example of the Arrogance Cycle. Millions of homeowners went through it. As housing prices began rising, there was a healthy dose of disbelief or skepticism. "Yes, prices are rising all over, but this is my home, this is where I live, and I don't want to put it at risk." Then acceptance: "How can I argue? This isn't illusion, it's fact. Everyone's making money on this housing market. Why shouldn't I?" And finally capitulation: "All right, the money is available; I don't see how we can lose. The banks are eager to loan money, so let's take advantage of this market."

Feeding this cycle, of course, is profit. This is the really insidious part of the Arrogance Cycle. When someone with little or no real estate experience can get into the housing market and make a profit, that's when disbelief turns to acceptance. Cash is so compelling. The psychological underpinnings are all too clear. It's exactly what B. F. Skinner discovered at the dawn of behavioral psychology when he ran tests on animals, then humans, and learned that behavior is determined by the search for reward and avoidance of punishment. The reward: If I buy a house today that's worth $300,000, it could be worth $400,000 next year, and half a million the year after that. The punishment: I'm busting my hump working at my job with a salary that's hardly keeping up with inflation.

So the lure of positive reinforcement—profits!—drove arrogance inexorably upward. It always does. What was the point in arguing for reality? "Does it make sense," I would ask, "that the house worth $350,000 a year ago is now worth two million? Is it remotely possible that this trend will continue ad infinitum?" It doesn't matter a damn, does it? People are making money. If money is being made, it must be real and true and good and right and noble, and just—hell, it must be holy!

Where did the validating, ratifying effect of profit begin? Maybe it started when caveman Kog scammed caveman Zog out of a fresh wildebeest carcass by foretelling of great calamity for Zog should he keep that wildebeest. You have to believe that Kog garnered a little respect from the other cave folk for procuring such an effortless meal for all of the little Kogs. Then they probably wanted to know how he did it. What exactly did Kog say to Zog, and might it work for me?

It didn't make sense, and yet people believed it. (Did you believe it?) The other persuasive thing about market falsehoods is that they're built on half-truths. Prices haven't fallen to their original levels, so maybe part of the increase was warranted? Maybe.

What happened next is what happens in every Arrogance Cycle: We began to see the world through narrow prisms of partial truths. Profits provide positive reinforcement, even in defiance of common sense. Everyone believes and believes and believes. Bad news and criticism are discounted. Any small scrap of good news is celebrated and glorified. Those who come bearing messages of caution are shooed away.

Afterwards, of course, the reality sets in. "I knew it." "I was a total schmuck." "I should have realized." But by then, of course, the cycle is over.

And the next wave is about to begin.

It may be too late for you, however; you may have already lost your place at the table.

HOW WE LOOK AT MONEY

You won't find any two individuals who regard money in quite the same way. To some it represents power. To others it's the reward for hard work, innovation, or productivity. Money, as we all know, can be used for purely manipulative purposes, or it can serve philanthropy, charity, or good works. It intimidates some while creating anger and resentment in others; it can occasion joy and celebration (getting that raise, winning that lottery, placing a winning bet) or shame and humiliation (going into debt, losing a job, experiencing foreclosure).

If you had another $1,000,000 in your bank account right now, how would you feel? If you were declared bankrupt tomorrow, how would you feel? Depending on who you are, you are likely to give very different answers to those questions, but I can almost guarantee you would feel *something*. None of us is immune to the emotional wallops that are linked to money.

In *Atlas Shrugged*, one of the characters, Francisco d'Anconia, gives an impassioned speech in which he extols the unique power of money as a creative force.

> *If you ask me to name the proudest distinction of Americans, I would choose—because it contains all others—the fact that they were the people who created the phrase "to* make *money." No other language or nation had ever used these words before; men had always thought of wealth as a static quantity—to be seized, begged, inherited, shared, looted or obtained as a favor. Americans were the first to understand that wealth has to be created.*[7]

In his disquisition on the nature of money, d'Anconia deplores the way it is equated with evil. But at the same time, he's adamant about the limitations of money when it comes to creating character, purpose, or morality.

> *Money will not purchase happiness for the man who has no concept of what he wants: money will not give him a code of values, if he's evaded the knowledge of what to value, and it will not provide him with a purpose, if he's evaded the choice of what to seek. Money will not buy intelligence for the fool, or admiration for the coward, or respect for the incompetent.*

Ayn Rand saw the *creation* of wealth as a laudable accomplishment; money earned by such means is richly deserved, whereas the money inherited or won at the gambling table is nothing of the sort. "Money is the product of virtue," declares d'Anconia, "but it will not give you virtue and it will not redeem your vices."

In the era when this was written, the choices seemed obvious. Each of us was given the power to decide. To make money purposefully and honestly was "a proud distinction." In contrast, there was money obtained by other means, the kind that was seized, "begged, inherited, shared, looted or obtained as a favor." It looked like each one of us had a clear choice to make. We could *create* wealth, or we could rake in the money . . . by whatever means necessary.

But it's not quite so simple a choice. What Rand didn't have when she wrote these words was a nice big magnetic resonance imaging machine to view how the brain behaves in action. If she'd had access to some brain scans, as we do today, she might have second-guessed the question of how we actually make choices that relate to money matters.

YOUR BRAIN ON OVERDRIVE

Deep in the substrata of the brain, in a very small area near the connection to the spinal cord, you have a collection of neurons that produce the chemical dopamine. This is a pleasure drug. There's really no other way to describe it. When neurons release dopamine, it sprays out in all directions, sending a rewarding jolt of positive energy through your body.

In *Your Money and Your Brain: How the New Science of Neuroeconomics Can Help Make You Rich*, Jason Zweig provides some insight into how dopamine does its work, influencing the behavior of a typical investor. It turns out that you don't get any kick at all from your dopamine-releasing brain if you receive exactly what you expect. The rising of the sun every day is actually a pretty thrilling event, but because you *expect* that event, you don't get a daily early-morning rush of dopamine. What it takes is the occurrence of some *unexpected* gain. As one scientist explained to Zweig, "When a reward comes as a surprise, the dopamine neurons fire longer and stronger than they do in response to a reward that was signaled ahead of time. In a flash, the neurons go from firing 3 times a second to as often as 40 times per second."[8] Once you feel the surge of pleasure that comes from that unanticipated reward, the dopamine in your system motivates you to seek more.

Not only that, research also shows that your neurons retain a memory of the preestablished pattern, and they're prepared to go into a flurry of dopamine-releasing activity when there's a good chance of pleasure (reward!) in your future. If you get a charge out of winning big the first time around, the neurons in your brain begin saying, automatically, "Give me more of that charge. Feels great!"

If this sounds like the kind of pleasure-seeking pattern that ultimately leads to addiction, scientists are quick to assure us that it is. "Lay an MRI brain scan of a cocaine addict next to one of somebody who thinks he's about to make money, and the patterns of neurons firing in the two images are 'virtually right on top of each other,'" says Zweig, quoting Harvard Medical School neuroscientist Hans Breiter. "'You can't get a better bull's-eye hit than those two.'"[9]

Of course, this is a part of the brain that's beyond our conscious control, and such findings have interesting implications when it comes to explaining how we behave as investors. If you get into the market and win big (or win at all) on your first investment, the underside of your brain is going to be shooting out little dopamine signals that say, "Do it again!" And because dopamine is also signaling you to *go bigger* next time, for a larger hit, your pleasure in making *some* money is translated into actions that induce you to take bigger risks in the hope of making more.

Even if your first efforts are entrepreneurial, creative, productive—that is, virtuous in every sense that Rand describes—the rush of pleasure you get from making money becomes an unconscious stimulant. "That was pleasant," your brain says. "Now make more," says the dopamine. "You had a good hit. Now let's go out and get a bigger one."

Welcome to the addiction.

YOUR GAMBLING INSTINCTS

Still, the reasoning brain is not entirely dormant. Just as cool heads may prevail in some situations, most of us have superego voices that say things like, "Okay, but let's not steal," or, "I'd love to make a ton of dough but I'm not going to screw my buddy to get it." Dopamine is powerful and insidious, but it's no dictator, and we still have the power to control our actions. What it does affect, however, is our sense of logic. Psychologists have looked at this, too, and their findings are not encouraging.

One study was conducted with a group of students playing a very simple gambling game called Acey-Deucey. It's played with a normal deck of fifty-two cards. Three cards are placed on the table in front of you. The outside cards are faceup, and the one in the middle is facedown. Your task is to guess whether your card in the middle has a value in between the values of the other two cards. If the faceup cards have a big spread, chances are great that the middle card falls somewhere in between. If the value distance between the two outside cards is smaller, then of course you're taking a bigger risk if you bet the middle card has a value within the range of the flanking cards.

Example: If the faceup cards are a queen on one side and a four on the other, you'd be well within your rights to bet that the one in the middle falls somewhere in between (any card from a five to a jack would do it—a total of seven cards). On the other hand, if the middle card is flanked by a six and a deuce, there's a much smaller probability that your bet would pay off. (The card in the middle must be one of only three cards—a three, a four, or a five.)

It doesn't take long to get the hang of the game, and even if you're not a whiz at statistics, you can usually do pretty well if you bet conservatively. That is, go ahead and put on a big bet if the faceup cards are a queen and a four, but rein in your gambling instincts if the cards are a six and a deuce.

But how will you start to play the game if you have a steady string of "good luck"? That's the question. Will you start to get a bit cocky and begin betting more often on the narrow spreads? Or will you keep your wits about you and continue to calmly calculate the odds on each individual round without regard for how well you did before? In other words, can you consciously control your own arrogance if you begin to "feel lucky"?

This is precisely the question asked by several researchers at Notre Dame[10] who decided to test out their hypothesis that a winning streak in a computer-generated game of Acey-Deucey would lead to more reckless gambling. Their test subjects were young adults, eighteen to twenty-four years of age, who (the researchers acknowledge) are more apt to take risks than those in other age groups. The researchers wanted to make the incentives for winning as realistic as possible, so they offered cash prizes to the participants. During their introductory remarks, they told the students they would be participating in an "actual tournament" where they would "be using a computerized version of a card game called Acey-Deucey."[11] After describing the game and setting some parameters on the number of chips that could be bet on each hand, the rounds began. The three cards were displayed on the screen—two faceup and one facedown—and after each student made his or her bet, the middle card was flipped faceup and the word WIN or LOSE came up on the screen. The first round went for thirty hands.

What the participants had no way of guessing was that the computer was programmed, in the first round, to deliver a winning streak to some of the players. The frequency with which the middle card came up with a value in between those of the outer two cards beat the laws of probability. (The computer programming made this possible; it couldn't have been done with an ordinary deck of cards.) So some of the first-round players were indeed lucky, and they had the winnings to show for it.

But for another group, the cards were rigged the other way. The odds were tipped *against* their winning—again, not blatantly, but with a higher-than-normal probability. So at the end of the first round, researchers had two distinct groups they could compare—the "Initial-Winning" and the "Initial-Losing" participants.

Question was, how would these two groups compare in their behavior during a second round when the cards were *not* rigged? Would the Initial Winners, flush with victory, begin to play more recklessly than they should? And, in round two, how would their betting measure up against participants who had been in the Initial Losers group?

As it turned out, the participants who had been on a winning streak in the first round (the Initial Winners) were indeed more reckless in their gambling in the second round. When the probability of winning was below 50 percent, Initial Winners went ahead and placed "inappropriately high bets," taking significantly more risk than the participants in the Initial Losers group.

In all other respects (i.e., their range of card-playing experience and gender mix), the groups were identical in makeup. The only difference was their experience in that first round. Initial Winners *felt* like winners, and it obviously went to their heads. And in round two, Initial Losers, humbled by their first losses, had no judgment impairment. They harbored no delusions that Lady Luck was on their side.

THE NOISE OF OTHER PEOPLE WINNING

There's another big factor influencing our investment behavior, and this also skews our performance. In addition to our personal illusions about the power of Lady Luck, most of us are vulnerable to outside influences. The sight, sound, or rumor of other people winning is a fierce stimulant to action. It's one thing if the grass is greener on the other side and you never see the grass. That, at least, is bearable. But when others just like you are winning, and you're not, it creates an almost irresistible pressure to take action. Naturally, psychologists have taken the time to study this phenomenon, and the results are most interesting.

In a study that intentionally selected frequent gamblers, conducted by researchers in Queensland, Australia, the subjects were put in front of gaming machines and told to go ahead and play to their hearts' content.[12] But unknown to the subjects, they were in two different playing environments. Those in group one played without any outside feedback signifying how others were doing. The subjects in group two did get feedback (which—known only to the testers—was faked); they heard winning bells and instant messages telling them other players in another room were winning big-time. Sure enough, the players who thought other people were winning fast and furiously placed more bets, and lost more money, than those who played without that feedback.

In 2000, I was handling the investments of a leading political commentator who was feeling tremendous remorse because he had just missed out on the whole dot-com boom. He had many friends who had made a whole lot of money, the NASDAQ was soaring, and he was kicking himself for not getting in earlier. Now he wanted to put 100 percent of his money in tech stocks. He felt he just had to *do something*. We argued. The tech market, at that point, reminded me of what had happened in 1915 when the new technology was cars, and there were 150 car companies. How many of those car companies survived? How many dot-coms were going to make it—and which ones? History suggested that 85 percent of the new dot-coms would disappear completely. It made absolutely no sense for him to get into that market, much less put all his savings into tech stocks.

At first, he decided to try it my way (and his wife agreed with me). So he put his money in bonds and a diversified portfolio of blue-chip stocks, and the market dropped for the next three years. I pointed out to him that our losses during those three years were less than the market. The market went down 10 percent. We went down less, but even so, he couldn't stand it. He was hearing from some guys who said the money was being made in private equities and municipal bonds. Reluctantly (because we were friends), and with many expressions of regret (but he really couldn't help himself), that's where he put his money.

Was it the right move? As it turned out, absolutely not. He was putting his money into an illiquid market at just that time of his life (age sixty) when he needed to do the opposite. But the point is, he felt he had to *do something*. He was listening to all the bells ringing and the cheers as others made money. He felt left behind. And when that happens, we'd rather make some move, even if it's inexplicable, rather than do nothing at all.

Yes, we all feel that way sometimes—and with good reason. But when you feel you have to do something just for the sake of action, I advise that you don't do it with your life savings. As one sage advisor suggested to me, "Go home, rearrange the furniture, clean the garage, sort out your sock drawer. You'll make some mistakes in judgment, but they're not as big as the mistakes you'll make with your money."

YOUR INVESTMENT BEHAVIOR

So . . . we have dopamine. We have the gambling instinct. And we have the noise of other people winning. All three have an influence on our behavior. Combined, they contribute mightily to an arrogant mind-set.

After that, only two conditions are required to create the environment where people can exercise their natural inclination to make money. First, we need the opportunities. A poker player needs his poker game. A gambler needs his Las Vegas. The entrepreneur needs an open market where she can sell her goods, and an investor needs the corporations or properties in which he can make his investment. Secondly, we need access to money—either in the form of cash or credit—before the dice can begin to roll or the machines of production can be put in motion.

During the nineties and in the early years of the new millennium, both criteria were met for the average investor (including the eager young sons of that housekeeper I mentioned earlier). Essentially, everything was in place for enthusiastic participation. There was the housing market, where prices had been steadily rising throughout history, making it appear that a homeowner's investment in real estate was a no-lose proposition, and there was access to the stock market, which over the long term had steadily and reliably edged upward. As corporations and employers began pushing employees off pension plans and into investment programs that were linked to market results, an ever-swelling number of Americans was becoming intimately familiar with market trends and increasingly reliant on a healthy market to meet their future living requirements.

And then along came a surge of creativity among market makers who created new products designed to take advantage of ever-increasing opportunities in a milieu in which there was ever-decreasing regulatory oversight. Within approximately a twenty-year span, as hedge funds were launched, investment trusts were created, and the derivatives market reached ever-higher levels of profitability, we would see the creation of more investment products than ever before. Each was designed to sop up the liquidity that was in abundant supply, thanks to the soaring equity in the housing market (which people could and did borrow against) and the ever-rising limits of unsecured credit. When the banks' leverage limits were lifted, everything was in place to create the illusion of an unlimited money supply.

WHEN OPPORTUNITY KNOCKS LOUDLY

Investors responded with enthusiasm to all these opportunities. The first signs of change in the housing market occurred when homeowners began to regard their properties as more than homes. The change in attitude was subtle at first, but soon became blatant. Buying a home, it was said, was "the best investment you can make." That observation appeared to be true, first, because it was a tangible asset that could be insured against loss; second, because, historically, housing prices went nowhere but up; third, because there was the tax benefit of a write-off on the mortgage; and fourth, because a homeowner could, after thirty or forty years, sell a home that was in the clear (mortgage-wise) and realize pure profit. As a sound personal investment for an individual or family, owning a house couldn't be beat.

But somewhere in the mid-eighties, as housing prices took off, along came a change in attitude among millions of home buyers. More and more, like the housekeeper's kids, we started to see our houses as an investment property as well as a place to call home. Census figures for 1999–2000, for instance, showed that about 16 percent of the population or 43 million Americans moved to new homes.[13] So they were all shoppers. In addition, many upwardly mobile families realistically regard a newly purchased house as a temporary shelter rather than permanent lodging. But when housing prices took off, even those who remained stationary began to feel like they could become smart investors if they bought low, improved the property, sold high, then reinvested in a new and bigger house that was sure to have even greater value the following year. As long as you were "buying up," as long as mortgages and closing costs remained fairly stable, and as long as your earnings were steady or increasing, this was a very smart investment. For many families, it was the largest they would ever make. And it was endorsed by the chairman of the Federal Reserve himself, Alan Greenspan. Not only did "Yoda," as he was often called, leave interest rates at or below 2 percent for three years, but he also encouraged people to take low-cost adjustable-rate mortgages as a great way to enhance "affordability."

Greenspan knew it all. He was clear that there was *not* a bubble in housing prices. His studies showed that real estate markets— and pricing—were regional.

Greenspan asserted that while there may be pockets of excessive valuations in different parts of the country, there was certainly *not* a national real estate bubble! Big Al didn't stop there. He said that low-interest-rate adjustable mortgages were sound, and he encouraged buyers to take advantage of these very low introductory rates.

Housing prices never stopped climbing in the eighties and nineties. The median price of a house in the United States in 1980 was $64,600. By the year 2000 that price had shot up to $169,000, during a period of low annual inflation.[14] And fixed-rate mortgages—which peaked as high as 16 percent in 1980— fell steadily to about 8 percent by the year 2000.[15] So, indeed, all the conditions were in place to continue feeding what Yale Economics professor Robert Shiller called the "irrational exuberance" in the housing market.

Initially, this was no bubble. As an ever-increasing number of homeowners got wise to the investment possibilities and began searching for new opportunities, there was real demand. A lot of people were making very sound investments that, within two or three or four years, would look extremely good on paper (even if they didn't sell right away). Buy a house in 1980 for $65,000, and within ten years its price had doubled. And it was a government-encouraged process, since there was a write-off on the mortgage interest and no capital-gains penalty for selling one house, as long as you were "buying up" to another.

But let's not forget that little part of the brain that sends out thrill signals when we win. There were not just houses in this market—there was dopamine. And as homeowners began winning with their investments, they began looking for other, and better, opportunities to experience that thrill again. Millions of American homeowners were discovering how good it felt to get richer day by day.

MORE REWARDS

Meanwhile, on a second front, an increasing proportion of American consumers were coming to see themselves as active investors. Many corporations were selling to their employees the idea that they would be far better off in retirement if they put a proportion of their earnings into 401(k) retirement accounts. In selling these "improved" retirement plans, forward-looking companies (with earnings-conscious accountants) could easily "prove" that such plans made sense. One had only to look at market indices for the previous twenty or thirty years to see that the stock market had climbed steadily, and assuming that growth continued, anyone with an index-linked portfolio was likely to prosper. Never mind that pesky legal disclaimer that "past performance is unreliable and no indication of future results." To make the deal even better, most companies proffered a "match" to whatever the employees put in, not only sweetening the deal, but making the point that the company was also investing in the employee's future well-being.

This all seemed to work well at first. Combined with the burgeoning of Individual Retirement Accounts, beginning in 1975, and 401(k) plans, beginning in the early 1980s, there was an explosion in investments by consumers. In 1984, three years after the 401(k)s were launched, there were 7.5 million participants and about 17,000 plans. By 2000, over 32 million employees were participating in some 330,000 plans,[16] and by 2008 the number of total participants had risen to 65 million, with some $3 trillion invested.[17]

At the same time that employees were encouraged to put their savings into 401(k)s and IRAs, many were pressed to show company loyalty by investing in the very companies they worked for. In places like Enron, employees who had drunk the Kool-Aid were putting their entire future savings into company stock. (My grandfather Michael F. Keogh used to tell me that you should never invest money in the stock market that you couldn't afford to lose. Pop-Pop's advice haunts me as I think about the millions of people who have invested their retirement savings there.)

And then came the dopamine. Employees relished reading the quarterly results of their "investments." The market was booming, and as the market boomed, indices rose. Though there were occasional years when setbacks occurred, for the most part the earnings looked secure. True, investor-employees with 401(k)s could not tap into those earnings until retirement without incurring a tax penalty, but that was the whole idea—to build an "untouchable" nest egg that would grow rapidly, preparing for the day when you would retire and have to live on a fixed income.

This, then, was another source of dopamine rushes. Every quarter, it was "Open the envelope, please," and "Who's the lucky winner?" What would the next report look like? How big would it be? But while our neurons were getting excited, again, reason faltered. The first thing we failed to notice was the way our retirement savings had become part of an overheated market. This was no old-fashioned pension plan where a certain percentage of salary was guaranteed to the retiree after age sixty-five. Nor was it an even older-fashioned savings account backed up by the FDIC. As the market soared, few amateur investors thought about what they needed to do to protect the assets upon which their future depended.

MORTGAGE-BACKED SECURITY?

We were winning on all fronts, and it felt good. We didn't know where the next big hit would come from—the goosed-up housing prices or the satisfying 401(k) reports—but just the expectation of more good news made us a bit giddy with the feeling that Lady Luck was with us. The full flush of egomaniacal arrogance was upon us.

At the same time, numerous incentives drove investment bankers and hedge fund managers to create products that would sop up ready money in circulation and lure the adventurous into new territory. Of course, for inventiveness to reign there had to be a nonrestrictive atmosphere, but the Reagan and Clinton administrations seemed to be on the same wavelength when it came to freeing the markets from restrictions. As words like *oversight* and *transparency* gradually lost their gravitas, trust was placed in those who seemed to know what they were doing. And if they produced results that were too good to believe, well, there was enough dopamine in circulation to clear the way for ever-more-exciting new products.

To most homeowners the news that their mortgages were being bundled up and sold off like so many job lots was a curiosity rather than a source of concern. When we learned that our mortgages were no longer held by the local bank—that, instead, they were collected into tranches of mortgage-backed securities that were then sold to Wall Street investors—we were unfazed. It all sounded kind of important. Our original deal with the bank or mortgage lender remained, on the surface, just the same as it had always been. The monthly payments might be made to a new entity with a different address, or you might go on making payments to your original lender as before, but in either case, you weren't called to the office for a rewrite of your mortgage agreement.

Yet something was beginning to change. Homeowners' mortgages were rapidly becoming part of a vast new machinery. Each individual mortgage was one cog in the wheels that were turning to produce unimaginable sums of money for aggressive investors. We were there at the birth of a new creation that would ultimately reap billions of dollars for Wall Street banks, but not one homeowner was asked for permission to use his monthly payments in this way, nor were we invited to the table when the winnings were shared among people who traded, swapped, insured, and leveraged those mortgage-backed securities.

What does it take to invent a new financial "product"? The inventor needs to be persuasive in order to convince others that the new product will, in fact, "work," that it will ultimately (in the short term or long term) prove profitable. In addition, there needs to be enough interest in the new product to draw in capital investment. And then there have to be buyers (the more, the better). Remember our cavemen: Kog may be a great storyteller, but unless Zog has a wildebeest, Kog's just wasting his breath. Finally, the financial inventors need to be operating in a climate where innovation is encouraged.

As it happened, all these conditions were in place in 1977[18] when Bank of America produced the first private-label mortgage-backed security. Fannie Mae and Freddie Mac soon followed suit (in 1981 and 1983, respectively). The first experiments proved more successful than its inventors could have dreamed. Before we knew it, millions of American homeowners, without explicit consent, were contributing to Wall Street's greatest new product.

Of course, what made this new product so beautiful at first was the fact that we homeowners were so incredibly reliable.

When Moody's and Standard & Poor's gave triple-A ratings to the first batches of mortgage-backed securities, the credit rating agencies were largely justified in their expression of confidence. The underlying assets were all those homes occupied by families across America. For the most part those homes were highly valued by their owners, who worked assiduously to meet their monthly payments. It would have been hard to find a more reliable group of conscientious contributors anywhere on the continent. We liked the concept of owning our own homes—even if we had to take out hefty mortgages to do it—and we were highly motivated to continue making the payments necessary to hold on to what we valued.

Even the mortgage-backed securities loaded up with adjustable-rate mortgages were, at least at the outset, supported by homeowners acting in good faith. True, many of them could have been more concerned about what would happen when their mortgage payments were adjusted upward at some future date. But there were many reasons for confidence. Home buyers assumed there would be a steady rise in home values. They were a sincerely optimistic bunch. I'm sure most of them believed their future earnings would increase to meet higher monthly payments. Initially, there was good faith all around. Solid credit ratings seemed justified. The new invention appeared to be as sound as it was clever.

But then . . . the dopamine kicked in, launching a cycle of arrogance like none other in recent memory.

Where the Money Came From . . .
and Where It Went

The beautiful credit history of American homeowners gave Wall Street a lot to work with. Banks that originated the mortgages continued to get income from servicing the loans. The creator of the mortgage-backed security (along with some variations of same) got a fee for putting the deal together. After those expenses were covered, the holder of the securities got steady income from all those people paying their monthly bills.

Geographical diversification helped spread the risk. As long as the securities were comprised of mortgages from different parts of the country, the risks of default seemed remote. Even if workers in Detroit were laid off and could no longer pay their mortgages, homeowners in Miami and L.A. and Boston would be unaffected. So, theoretically, a security made up of mortgages from all these places would remain sound. Still, there was the very remote chance that a slump in the economy would result in widespread unemployment, and if that happened, yes, it was possible that a significant proportion of homeowners would be unable to meet their payments.

To hedge against this eventuality, yet another product was invented—the form of insurance that would ultimately become notorious, the Credit Default Swap. The elegance of this invention was the way it alleviated the ultimate risk and responsibility and consequence of default from the bond purchaser to the insurer. No one thought that pools of mortgages would, as a group, totally default, so insurers wrote this insurance for pennies and thought they were stealing as they collected their premiums. Talk about arrogance! Talk about *wrong!*

But a really huge insurer, AIG, was pleased to rake in fees on all those "risk-free" loans. AIG was the largest purveyor of credit default swaps. Their institutional dopamine made them believe that taking fees for this sort of "doomsday" insurance was laughable. They couldn't write enough of it. Meanwhile, back on the home front, most homeowners steadily kept up their end of the bargain. To the best of our ability, we made those monthly payments, and we made them on time. Sure, there were some late payments, and every once in a while, a home was lost through foreclosure if Mom or Dad lost a job, for instance, or if some uninsured (or underinsured) member of the family racked up huge hospital bills. But the vast majority of homeowners was reliable and was expected to remain so.

What they couldn't control, however, was the investment edifice built upon their reliability. Now it was not just a local banker or the mortgage originator who depended on the homeowner's monthly payment; a lot more was at stake. There were all those investors who had bought the bundles of mortgages and, further up the line, many other banks, investors, and insurers who shared the risk. This was a lot of financial superstructure to place on the shoulders of homeowners. If anything went seriously wrong and a whole lot of homeowners suddenly found themselves unable to meet their monthly payments, the edifice would tilt, or worse, collapse.

TILT!

Several years into the new millennium, the cracks started to appear. In the euphoria of the times, with home prices rising, mortgage rates at new lows, and new mortgages being generated at an unprecedented rate, few wanted to acknowledge that the scaffold was getting rickety. But the signs were there.

In fact, in their haste to take advantage of the new products that the geniuses on Wall Street had created, people forgot the premise upon which the whole structure had been built. The mortgages were only reliable *if* conscientious homeowners could afford to meet their monthly obligations. As the housing market heated up, the issuers of mortgages stretched their definition of who was a worthy home buyer. Driven by huge incentives to find more sources of mortgages, lenders like Countrywide Finance were eager to enlist buyers who would sign up willingly, whatever their creditworthiness or employment histories.

In the first wave of fervent creation of mortgage-backed securities, homeowners had been passive contributors. Each mortgage had become one cog in the wheels of investment machinery. Now, however, the rising tide was creating demand. The individual home buyer became a target of ever-sweeter offers. Adjustable Rate Mortgages with extremely low starter rates became the rage, and mortgages could be had for no money down. In some cases, the stars of this arrogant new marketing blitz did away with details like credit or employment checks. They needed to generate new mortgages to feed the investment beast as urgently as potential home buyers wanted new or larger homes. They championed the theory that no matter how bad the credit of the home buyer, if you collected enough of them (without regard to their ability to service the debt, much less repay the principal) and spread them around geographically, you could mitigate risk and get away with a triple-A rating on your new bonds. This is akin to the idea that some of our fish may be spoiled, but if we sell it by the ton, it can't all be bad, and who's going to figure it out anyway?

The infection had spread to become an epidemic. Wall Street buzzed with the arrogance of the bankers and investors who believed they couldn't lose. In the mortgage factories—including the gargantuan Fannie Mae and Freddie Mac, as well as relatively new arrivals like Countrywide—there was the arrogant belief that rising demand and soaring prices would continue for eternity. And newly created among home buyers was the arrogance of being in a can't-lose situation. A house was still the best investment you could make. The market was steadily rising. Every homeowner had, essentially, become an investor. And every investor was a winner. The Arrogance Cycle was at full throttle.

CHAPTER 3

PYRITE

Arrogantly Gullible

Bernie Madoff is a world-class, no-good son of a bitch (which is probably insulting to world-class, no-good sons of bitches everywhere!). He is among the worst human beings imaginable. He was filthy rich, arrogant, confident, charming, brilliant—and he was a thief. Madoff took "members only" exclusivity to an all-time low. Should he have been caught much, much earlier than he was? Could anyone have known? *Yes!* The evidence was ample.

As far as I know, his club never had a slogan, but it should have: "Only the arrogant need apply." Only those who believe that they have the right to belong to an inside group that holds the secret key to the City of Gold. Only the true believers, who will never lose faith in the genius who runs the club. Only those who have the arrogance to think the rest of us are just totally clueless.

The trouble with the City of Gold is that it's likely to be the City of Pyrite—fool's gold. Pyrite is iron sulfide; gold is a pure element. To some eyes they look alike. They're not.

How did it work? Some rich current client would offer to get you in. Prospects were less concerned with the details than they were with the thought of being left out of the profitable parade. New investors understood that the superior returns depended on the brilliant Madoff sharing his one-of-a-kind, wildly winning formula. Newbies wouldn't dare question the great and powerful Oz. There was also the presumption that anything as marvelously successful had to be more complicated than an average investor could possibly fathom. (The fear of looking stupid quashes a lot of good questions.) And then there was the camaraderie, the knowing smile, the nod of recognition when you *belonged* and you met someone else who also belonged.

"You know Bernie?"

"Sure. Great guy."

"He sure is."

"You betcha."

Afterwards, the members of that club couldn't believe how they'd had the wool pulled over their eyes. They were aghast at the nerve, the duplicity, the amorality of the guy. What was he—some kind of sociopath? How could he screw his "friends" like that? Old folks, families, widows, charities—didn't matter to Bernie. His philosophy, as he later revealed to his prison mates, was quite simple: "Screw 'em." And that's what he proceeded to do. Over and over and over again, for thirty-five years, a Ponzi scheme that deep-sixed an estimated $65 billion of "investments" from the folks who were suckered in.

Much of the vanishing money belonged to philanthropic organizations around the world. The Madoff vacuum was not just left in account balances and in the lives and living standards of the once-wealthy, but also in the plethora of charitable services that those funds once secured.

We are equally desperate to defend our arrogant mistakes as being reasonable or at least justifiable. The rationalizing, like the arrogance, knows few boundaries. The "It's too complicated" argument is common. Many will prefer cloaking *too complicated* in more intricate, emphatic language, like "The vast complexity rendered the offering nearly imponderable, almost demanding expert counsel." The point is not to feel bad about having done something unjustifiably idiotic. *All of that heavy-duty financial stuff is way over my head. I can't possibly understand it, so DON'T BLAME ME for the disastrous outcome.*

So there you have it. The zenith of extreme arrogance and the nadir of human character. It probably doesn't get much worse than Bernie. On the other hand, it would be foolhardy to believe that the kind of sociopathic, criminal negligence displayed by Madoff is the only kind of arrogance that extracts a cost from society and shatters the confidence of investors. In the culture of "I Deserve It," extreme arrogance takes many forms. We ignore the signs at our own peril.

SURE SIGNS OF EXTREME ARROGANCE

What are the signs of extreme arrogance? There are a number of strong signals that should get your antennae waving.

One is competitive overdrive. Most of us are competitive by nature, and where there is money involved, the appetite for victory can become particularly voracious. Sports analogies pervade the investment world, and there's a reason. Take a big profit—on paper or in cash—and it feels like winning a hard-fought game. Make a great investment or get a windfall, and before you know it, you're championship material. Great feeling. Fine; enjoy it. But when it goes to extremes, you know you've got a problem. When you see guys who will do anything to win, beware. They'll flex the rules. Twist the rules. Break the rules. That's when extreme, amoral arrogance takes over. Technically, that level of arrogance may not be illegal. After all, there are often loopholes in the law. But mere legality doesn't change the nature of amoral arrogance: It's still a grave offense.

When competitiveness reaches the point where it's the sole driving force behind a corporate culture, we have another kind of arrogance problem. Rule benders and rule breakers, surrounded by like-minded colleagues, experience the kind of reinforcement that encourages them to push the boundaries, take greater risks, ignore the consequences. During the first decade of the new millennium, we saw some of the biggest Wall Street firms transformed into hothouses where this kind of groupthink prevailed. The outcome was not only corporate recklessness but also a sense of rightness and invulnerability that was reinforced by peers, confreres, and colleagues who flourished in the same environment.

Of course, in these kinds of cultures—as in any club of high achievers—there's a monumental assumption of mental superiority. *We're winning. We belong to a club where everyone's winning. We must be geniuses. How else to explain it? We're smarter than the other guys. We're more inventive. We're quicker. We're more clever. We're not arrogant. We're just brighter than anyone else.*

A broker I'll call Syl Slickboy interviewed with me not long ago. He was chortling over his days as an institutional broker for the regional brokerage firm of Makem Bleede & Mohn. His language, which I won't bother repeating verbatim, was strewn with the usual four-letter words. But the gist of it was this: "They'd be doing some rotten deal that none of us wanted to sell," Slickboy explained to me, "and Makem would walk out on the floor and pick out some poor guy not on his phone and start yelling at him. 'Smith! What are you doing? Do you work for MBM? Does MBM write your paycheck? Get your ass on that phone and sell whatever the hell MBM tells you to sell to MBM's clients. These aren't your clients—they're ours. If you don't want to work here, call Merrill Effing Lynch. If you do want to work here, *get your ass on that phone and start selling!*' It was unbelievable," Slickboy told me, laughing. "It was a total circus, but we did sell a lot of crap over the years."

Inevitably, the combination of competitiveness mixed with a conviction of mental superiority creates another characteristic of extreme arrogance: hostility. *I'm quick and smart and competitive and clever. Those other guys are idiots. Look how easy it is to fool them. I can make them believe anything. I say, "Your house is worth twice as much as it was two years ago," and they believe it. I say, "This market can only go up," and lo and behold, they really believe this market can only go up. I tell them, "There's no downside to this investment," and incredibly enough, they fall for it. "I'll bet I could tell them they can live forever." There's no limit to gullibility.* When the extremely arrogant think and speak and e-mail disparagingly of their own clients, this is what they're thinking.

Yet another factor in extreme arrogance is the uncontrolled and usually unstoppable yearning for more. Though commonly labeled *greed,* that word does not quite encompass what occurs when extreme arrogance reaches its peak. What begins as an insatiable appetite for money (and everything else) is transmogrified into a necessity for the accretion of wealth for recognition. More money spells superior ability. There is a need for validation precisely because true substance is so absent. "You may think I'm full of crap, but I just got paid ten million dollars for being full of it. So whaddya think about *that?*"

But when the veneer is so thin, there is never enough validation. If you or I received a $10 million bonus last year and then got another $10 million bonus this year, there's a good chance we would feel grateful. To those in the club of extreme arrogance, it's impossible to feel that way. *Grateful?* For getting *this* year exactly what I got *last* year? That's what's called being stuck in a rut. To the extremely arrogant, there *has* to be more. Not just because they need it. There must always be more because they believe they're *worth* more—and that dollar figure is the all-important measurement of their worth.

And this is where arrogance reaches the ultimate extreme—when there is no longer any line between what a person needs and what he or she will do to get it. Those who reach the peak of extreme arrogance—from the bonus-saturated CEOs of failing companies to the Bernie Madoffs wielding their Ponzi schemes—are not defined by their lifestyles, their assets, or their appetites. They are defined by the way they create their own rules that apply only to themselves.

DELUSIONS OF GREATNESS

When Muhammad Ali announced "I am the greatest!" he set a standard that many arrogant young men and women on Wall Street have aspired to match. Announcements like this have become everyday occurrences. In part, this is bluster, the natural outcome of great egos nurtured by early and easy winnings. But many of those who believe or announce their greatness have the same motivation as the self-promoting champ of world boxing—to live out their own myth of themselves.

Hypercompetitiveness may be beneficial for a sports champion, but it does strange things to men and women who are entrusted with other people's money. How does it change them? What's the transition from cleverness and ingenuity—decent traits in and of themselves—to high levels of arrogance?

The "inside story" of one such transition—within the highly respected Wall Street firm of J.P. Morgan—is well told by *Financial Times* writer Gillian Tett.[19] Portions of that tale are worth repeating here. Though J.P. Morgan was one of the firms left standing at the end of the credit default crisis, its deep involvement took the firm to the brink of collapse.

The saga began in the early 1990s when J.P. Morgan seemed to be falling far behind other Wall Street hotshot firms like Salomon Brothers, Goldman Sachs, and Bankers Trust. The problem was not caused by a shortage of young men eager to work hard. In that department, J.P. Morgan had the cream of the crop. Nor was it lack of clout. J.P. Morgan was a huge firm with international reach and a grand reputation throughout the world. The problem was not even profitability. In the early nineties, J.P. Morgan was doing well, but in terms of profitability and innovation it was outstripped by many of the other firms. By the kill-or-be-killed measures of Wall Street, J.P. Morgan was getting killed.

Within J.P. Morgan, a small band of pioneers, initially led by Peter Hancock, set out to remedy this situation. What he chose as an arena for battle was derivatives trading. It was a logical choice with room for expansion, albeit with many risks. Hancock and his team felt like they were up to the challenge, and in the early going, there were many signs they were right. The derivatives market was exploding. It had been started in the 1980s by a number of well-established investment banks, and though the market was scarcely understood by many traders and brokers, derivatives contracts proliferated wildly in the nineties. At J.P. Morgan alone, the derivatives activity reported in 1992 was $512 million; two years later, the estimated value of all the derivatives contracts was in the range of $1.7 trillion.[20] Regulators had not yet stepped in, and in an atmosphere where the prevailing attitude was that markets could regulate themselves, there seemed little risk that the SEC would put an end to the party. Clearly, J.P. Morgan already had a foot in the door, and Hancock was determined to make the firm a leader. Given the reputation of J.P. Morgan and the weight its name carried on Wall Street, if Hancock created the right derivatives products, he could leave the competition in the dust. All he needed was a great team to produce world-beating ideas. His group was young, bright, and dynamic, with just the right combination of eager recklessness and hard-driving work ethic needed to make it sing. As Tett describes the team, "[T]hey were all convinced, with the heady arrogance of youth, that they held the secret to transforming the financial world, as well as dramatically enhancing J.P. Morgan's profit profile."[21]

Though derivatives trading is widely regarded as a newfangled and nearly incomprehensible form of investment, it is based on a simple principle that dates back to the early days of commerce. If I agree to pay you $50 today for a bushel of wheat, that's a simple exchange of money for goods. In derivatives trading, we add a time element that makes the exchange more complicated. In a futures deal (the simplest kind of contract), I agree that I'll pay you $50 for a bushel of wheat *six months from now*. Since the price of wheat may go up or down in the next six months, you're taking a risk by accepting my offer, and you put a price on that risk. You say, "Okay, if you pay me $2 *today,* I'll agree to sell you that bushel of wheat for $50 six months from now." Now, three things can happen six months from now: The price of wheat (on the market) could be higher, it could be lower, or it could be the same.

If it's lower, you keep the $2, and I buy cheaper wheat at the lower market price. You won't get $50, but you'll have whatever the market price is then, plus my $2. You're happy to be $2 ahead of the market price, and I'm happy to buy wheat at less than $50. Your side of the transaction would be called a *hedge*—you were hedging against lower prices. But there's a risk that the price of wheat could go higher, that you'd have to sell it to me at $50. With the $2 I paid for the contract, you net $52—not bad. If the market price is $60, I feel good because I've saved myself $8 per bushel, and you still got $2 more than the then-$50 market price. All contracts like this are designed to limit one's perceived risk and to provide some level of insurance. Makes sense, if you're dealing in a commodity like wheat.

By the early 1990s, however, derivatives had become infinitely more complicated. Indeed, many of these trades were beyond the understanding of most of the human race. The trade could be an option (rather than an obligation) to buy or sell. The underlying "good" could be foreign currency, a bond, a security, or a Treasury bill. Even more esoterically, it could even be a debt obligation. If all was going well, each of those derivatives—which was really a contract for a future exchange—could be regarded as leverage for potential income. But if the market moved in ways that made the contract worse, then at some point the party that generated the derivative contract would have to settle its accounts, register its losses, lick its wounds, and move on.

Within Hancock's team there was intense competitive pressure to come up with new derivative products, or, indeed, to so alter the way business was being done that competitor banks would never catch up. They began to scrutinize a new generation of derivatives, called *swaps*. They realized that it might be possible—with certain kinds of derivative contracts—to arrange a "swap" between an investor holding one kind of contract and an investor holding another. If both were willing to pay a fee for the swap, then the deal-maker—in this case, J.P. Morgan—would make money coming and going. All they had to do was find parties that were mutually interested in doing this kind of deal and bring them together.

Of course, some of the interested parties would be doing these transactions as a real hedge against the rise and fall in future prices, as had long been done in the commodities markets, and for them the transaction could be considered an investment. But others would be doing these transactions purely to see what kind of profit they could make. To the dealer in the middle, it didn't matter what the motive was. Either way, if there was a buyer and a seller, the deal got done and a commission was paid to the middleman. J.P. Morgan wanted to be a big, big middleman.

As Tett points out, Hancock and his team were not trailblazers when it came to inventing swaps. A trader at Salomon Brothers engineered what was probably the first swap in 1981. It was an exchange that applied to currencies. IBM was holding bonds in Swiss francs and German deutsche marks, but wanted to get cash in dollars. The World Bank, meanwhile, held bonds that were denominated in dollars, but needed to diversify into other currencies, like francs and deutsche marks. With Salomon Brothers acting as the go-between, and collecting a commission, a swap was arranged so that IBM's earnings in marks and francs (on the bonds held by IBM) would go to the World Bank, while the World Bank's earnings on *its* bonds would go (in the form of dollars) to IBM. Both organizations got what they wanted, even though no actual trade occurred, and for its role Salomon Brothers earned $210 million.[22]

"This new form of trade," says Tett, "quickly spread across Wall Street and the City of London, mutating into wildly complex deals that seemed to give bankers godlike powers. With derivatives, they could take existing assets or contracts apart and write contracts that reassembled them in entirely new ways, earning huge fees."

J.P. Morgan's traders saw unlimited opportunity. With the company positioned as a market maker and its triple-A reputation to back up these deals, this looked like their chance to beat out the Salomon Brothers for the business. Tett likens the actions of the J.P. Morgan derivatives team to the pioneers of space travel— a "small group of brilliant minds" that was "charting the outer reaches of cyberfinance." To other insiders in the banking indus- try, this team was at the forefront of innovation and exploration, "solving the most foundational riddles of their discipline."[23]

Clearly, there was plenty of dopamine going around, with some to spare. From their gaming table within J.P. Morgan, the elite team felt like it was on a mission to change all the rules. And since Wall Street is a place where every trader is aware of all the clamor of other people winning every day, all the incentives were in place to compel this team to take ever-bigger risks.

It was a heady time—literally—as all their nerve endings responded to the addictive drug of profits . . . and more profits. For the Hancock team working at J.P. Morgan, the highlight of this market was credit derivatives deals. By 1999, when J.P. Morgan had cornered nearly half the market on credit derivatives, the total of official deals was around $229 billion. "The bank had not just kick-started the business," says Tett. "It virtually *was* the market."[24]

In celebrating its success, and as a courtesy to its best clients, the bank published a special edition of its own book, *The J.P. Morgan Guide to Credit Derivatives,* describing how J.P. Morgan was using uniquely advanced methods to measure and control the degree of risk associated with credit. "By separating specific aspects of credit risk from other risks," the book explained, "credit derivatives allow even the most illiquid credit exposures to be transferred to the most efficient holders of that risk."

Though J.P. Morgan had become the biggest player in the area of credit derivatives, its traders were keenly aware that the competition was still pulling ahead. Return on Investment (ROI) reported by J.P. Morgan in 1999 was a very healthy 19 percent. But banks like Chase Manhattan, Merrill Lynch, and Goldman Sachs were all reporting ROI over 20 percent—and, for the Bank of New York, the ROI was 34 percent.[25] Stock prices reflected the discrepancy. J.P. Morgan's stock doubled between 1997 and 2000—but at Merrill Lynch and Citigroup, share prices nearly tripled.[26]

The irony was that all of these firms were now in competitive overdrive, vying with each other to create products that were more exotic than their next-door neighbor's. In this atmosphere of extreme arrogance, they did not consider the consequences. Their goal was simply to invent and sell—harder than the other guys, more creatively than the other guys, and more convincingly than the other guys. A monster was being created, and re-created, behind closed doors, and every time someone else got a glimpse of the monster, they wanted in on its creation.

From her perspective as a *Financial Times* correspondent covering the credit markets, Tett saw it all happen.

As the losses piled up . . . some members of the team realized that certain assumptions that had driven them a decade before had been naive. Back in the 1990s the team had all believed, with near-evangelical fervor, that innovation would create a more robust and efficient financial world. Credit derivatives and CDOs [collateralized debt obligations], they assumed, would disperse risk. Now it turned out that the risks had not been dispersed at all, but concentrated and concealed. It was a terrible, horrible irony.[27]

In the land of theory, perhaps the principle of credit derivatives was completely sound. But in the eat-or-be-eaten environment of Wall Street, where ideas morphed into reality, those derivatives turned into what Warren Buffett called (in 2003) "time bombs" and "financial weapons of mass destruction" that could harm the whole financial system.[28]

How right he was.

AT THE FOREFRONT OF SELF-DESTRUCTION

You may remember Lehman Brothers. It wasn't the biggest firm on Wall Street and it wasn't the smallest, but as a corporate culture, it was surely one of the most arrogant. And in case you don't remember, just a quick recap: This was the firm that ran up $660 billion in debt,[29] mostly in markets that half the guys didn't understand. It was this 158-year-old investment bank which, in the early days of September 2008, on the brink of filing for Chapter 11 bankruptcy,[30] ran around asking, begging, pleading for government help in order to bail itself out of trouble. This was the firm that Henry Paulson, then secretary of the U.S. Treasury, declined to rescue from collapse.

Certainly the collapse of Lehman is a vivid memory for anyone who had much of their life savings in the stock market and who felt the tremors of a global financial collapse. On September 15, 2008, when Paulson declined to take measures to rescue the firm, and Lehman imploded, the Dow Jones Industrial Average plummeted 500 points.[31] It was a bankruptcy that, as one insider noted,[32] "was bigger than WorldCom, Enron, Conseco, Texaco, Refco, Washington Mutual, United Airlines, Delta, Global Crossing, Adelphia, Mirant, and Delphi combined."

Within forty-eight hours, the world financial markets were shuddering as the tremors of the bank's collapse created a tsunami of uncertainty that spread calamitously to all corners of the globe.[33]

Most of the European markets had been quivering as bad news about the American housing market and rumors of the imminent demise of the largest U.S. investment firms began to look like a potential meltdown of the complete American economy. Now, with the final expiration of Lehman Brothers, their worst fears were realized. The value of Germany's blue-chip stocks and France's top-forty companies sank more than 40 percent between May and September. As the fallout from Lehman spread around the continent, Spain's index sank more than 30 percent and Ireland's ISEQ—the official list of equities on the Dublin Exchange—lost more than half its value. In Iceland, soon to become a poster child of the worldwide financial collapse, citizens watched helplessly as the index of stocks fell below 677 from a May high of 4,942. London's FTSE sank to 3,873 from a May high of 6,300. Markets in Russia, China, Japan, Hong Kong, Australia, and Brazil were similarly shaken.[34]

If you had a 401(k) or an IRA, I'm sure you can recall the ghastly sinking feeling your stomach experienced as, in aggregate, trillions of dollars disappeared overnight. Is it all coming back now?

Well, the corporate culture that created the conditions for this wipeout was no ordinary place. This was a gathering of the elite, an exclusive club comprised of extremely bright young men and women. In the words of Lawrence McDonald (who worked there during those times), Lehman Brothers was a place for people "born and bred for Wall Street from the time they were infants." From private schools like Exeter, Andover, Choate, and St. Paul's, most of them had made a smooth transition to one of the Ivy Leagues or MIT, Northwestern, the University of North Carolina, or Duke. Many had done time in the Harvard, Sloan, or Wharton business schools. As one of the new entrants into this culture, McDonald observed: "[W]e were in the presence of gods, the new Masters of the Universe, a breed of financial daredevils who conjured Lehman's billion-dollar profits out of one of the most complex markets ever to show its head above Wall Street's ramparts."[35]

But this was not just an elitist firm where arrogance flourished. It was also a bunch of hard-driving (some might say rapacious), competitive-minded gamblers. The trading floors were like casinos, cool and well-oxygenated, an adrenaline-laced atmosphere for the ambitious young go-getters who were creating the world of the future.[36] Floors competed against floors, departments against departments. Daily postings kept the competitive hellions going after each other, and rumors bounced from trading desks to conference rooms like mercury escaping from a broken thermometer. When someone crashed, others gloated. When one person won, others envied and backstabbed. It was well known at Lehman that only the strong survived. Those who flourished took great pride in having the instincts of jungle animals.

Mind you, this was not a Mafia-like gang that set out to defraud the American public. On the contrary, the very concept of a "public" was so foreign to the traders and market-makers in the cocoons of their respective floors that, to them, most outsiders were beneath contempt. The Lehman culture was defined by competitiveness, and within that culture, it wasn't how or why you played the game that mattered, it was simply *who won*. Who got the biggest bonuses? Who one-upped the other guys? Who could show profits that would make the clowns at Bear Stearns look like a struggling JV team and make the traders at Goldman Sachs turn green with envy?

As the market heated up, at least some of the actors in the great Lehman drama were well aware of the potential for disaster, particularly when it came to the insanely upbeat assumptions that were being made about the housing market. After one particularly optimistic meeting, when everyone seemed to agree that housing prices could only go up, the head of high-yield and leveraged-loan businesses, Alex Kirk, confided, "The whole thing is fucking ridiculous . . . This market is on fucking steroids."[37] But such doubts were not leaked to other departments. Lehman Brothers was like any urban playground, and the brawling rival gangs did not disclose weakness. Within each department, loyalties were tight (so much so that when the company folded, tears were shed for the shattered camaraderie, for the casualties among the gang members). But these alliances—the mutual admiration societies and marriages of convenience—only contributed to divisiveness among rival factions. And above it all, up on the thirty-first floor, keeping distant watch over the brawlers below, was a management team as remote and—many claimed—as blissfully ignorant of the goings-on as a prison warden on an extended coffee break.

The capo, Dick Fuld, was a man who, before arriving at work in his limousine, made sure that someone radioed ahead so that a private elevator would be waiting for him on the ground floor, enabling him to be whisked up thirty-one stories without encountering any of his employees.[38] He worked with a tightly knit group of lieutenants who carried out his commands to the letter. Renowned for his well-honed ability to fire people at the least provocation, equally famous for his towering rages when crossed or offended, he was the boss who, in general, underlings did not want to meet.[39] Of course, it didn't help that he had little understanding of what occurred on the floors beneath him, where scrappy kids were trotting out the world's most passive-aggressive creations of personal aggrandizement and financial destruction. Fuld, McDonald noted, "had become separated from the most modern technology and the ultramodern trading of credit derivatives—CDO (collateralized debt obligations), RMBS (residential mortgage-backed securities), CLO (collateralized loan obligations), CDS (credit default swaps), and CMBS (commercial mortgage-backed securities)."[40]

Within Lehman were individuals like Kirk who could see the writing on the wall. But in a culture like this, you don't share the bad news unless there is a political advantage in doing so, and when upper management was announcing numbers that made Lehman Brothers look like a winner, woe betide the guy who stepped up to the plate to declare: "These numbers are bogus; these assumptions are wrong; this company is going to go bust."

In the end, though, that was the truth of the matter. The numbers created by the best talent on Wall Street were based upon shared perceptions that amounted to lies. The so-called assets recognized by the elite graduates of the world's finest universities were crap. And the firm renowned for its quickness, ingenuity, and valor proved to be the consummate beggar on the street. In Lehman's final days, its leaders went on their hands and knees to the U.S. Treasury secretary, scrounging for a handout that would save the firm, and when they were refused—when the pin was pulled and bankruptcy came crashing down—they suffered so deeply that some of them had to give up their boats and helicopters, move their children out of private schools, put their art collections up for auction, and even sacrifice beachfront property.[41]

As for the hit taken by retirees on fixed incomes, for the nest eggs and retirement accounts wiped out in the ensuing crash— well, perhaps a few at Lehman Brothers regretted their carnival ride on the Cyclone of extreme arrogance. But on September 15, as the doors closed on the Lehman Fight Club at 745 Fifth Avenue, most of them were too busy blaming each other for what had gone wrong to pause and consider the fate of the public that had been hauled to the peak of an edifice built of straw. In truth, to the bitter end, Lehman was all that mattered to the folks at Lehman. As one of the insiders mourned so poignantly, "I always stop and stare up at the floors where I'd found, I thought, the holy grail. Up there, behind the huge glass windows, we'd all fought it out, us against the world. . . . Even now I cannot quite understand what went wrong."[42] Alchemy relies on an arrogant, gullible audience to send money and chant "Amen."

MENSA MONSTERS AND FED CHAIRMEN

Some people claim that it's difficult to identify the qualities of genius, and perhaps that's so. But during the recent go-round in our economic cycle, it has been quite easy to identify the genius who stood head and shoulders above the rest. His name was Alan Greenspan, former chairman of the Federal Reserve (as if you could forget).

Ask anyone back then, and they would have told you: Greenspan was the wise sage with the godlike brow and the jowls of a prophet who kept a steady hand on the economy. The champion of theories of ebullient trade and open markets, a true believer with faith in the inherent checks and balances of the self-appointed, self-policing guardians of self-interest. An eloquent if somewhat abstruse observer who could render a pronouncement so delicately that his listeners could spend days, weeks, or months parsing its syllables and pondering its mystical, Yoda-esque meaning. He was held in high esteem. As Representative Jim Saxton, Republican from New Jersey, said to the Fed chairman in 2005, "You have guided monetary policy through stock-market crashes, wars, terrorist attacks and natural disasters. You have made a great contribution to the prosperity of the U.S. and the nation is in your debt."[43]

That was in 2005. Three years later, the encomiums from members of Congress were more muted.

True, the quality of genius was not all his. Al was surrounded by many others whose intellects seemed almost as towering. To them he occasionally turned, always privately, always discreetly, perhaps picking up some hints and tips now and then. But it was the Greenspan intellect that was the dominant force, and when he said such-and-such was so, we were strongly inclined to believe he knew all there was to know about such-and-such. Indeed.

"Debt leverage of all types is often troublesome when one judges the stability of the economy. Should home prices fall, we would have reason to be concerned about mortgage debt; but measures of household financial stress do not, at least to date, appear overly worrisome,"[44] he said, famously, on October 19, 2004, as the housing market heated up. "To be effective regulators, we must also attempt to balance the burdens imposed on banks with the regulations' success in obtaining the intended benefits and to discover permissible and more-efficient ways of doing so. Because we understand that regulatory changes can be quite costly, we recognize as well the important regulatory responsibility to balance the cost of change with the desired benefits," he orated on March 11, 2005, as, freed of regulation as well as liquidity requirements, the multitrillion-dollar derivatives market turned on the afterburners. "In this increasingly competitive and complex financial services market, it is essential that consumers acquire the knowledge that will enable them to evaluate products and services from competing providers and determine which best meet their long- and short-term needs,"[45] he announced at the height of the Arrogance Cycle, as bankers and traders up and down Wall Street were creating products that even the most knowledgeable investment gurus were at a loss to explain. But Alan Greenspan had an overarching philosophy that he held to, through thick and thin, despite the annoying details of a market where runaway arrogance prevailed. "In the broad sweep of history, it is ideas that matter. Indeed, the world is ruled by little else."[46]

But he couldn't have done it alone. Genius attracts genius, and all around him, he had men and women with bold vision and the courage of their pronouncements. (Meanwhile, far from the halls of power in Washington and the pinnacles of finance in New York, most of us were struggling to make our livings in the more-ordinary world of hourly wages and eroding salaries.) There was, for instance, Ben S. Bernanke, a member of the Federal Reserve Board when Greenspan was chairman, who opined, in 2005, that there really was no threat of a housing bubble that could burst: The 25 percent increase in house prices over the previous two years, he declared, was largely a reflection of "strong economic fundamentals."[47] Or the Fed's vice chairman, Roger W. Ferguson Jr., who clearly reflected the views of his captain when he told the Fourth Joint Central Bank Conference on Risk Management and Systemic Risk (Frankfurt, 2005) that "Making a case for early regulatory intervention is particularly difficult when the private parties involved in an innovation are sophisticated because, in many cases, they will be the first to recognize possible problems and will have strong incentives to fix them and also to protect themselves against fraud or unfair dealing."[48] It was reassuring to hear them speak, even if we did not quite understand what they were saying, because everyone seemed to agree that these guys were very, very smart, and we always want to know what the smart guys think.

Their elocution achieved the desired result. They were never wrong. Just ask them. Later, some admitted that they had misjudged. Others may have said they overlooked certain signs, or failed to pay enough attention to contributing factors. But when you're capable of great elocution, the one thing you never have to admit is that you've been stupid, that you've said some really dumb things, and because you're in a position of responsibility, really screwed things up. Geniuses don't say things like that. In the Mensa club, about as far as you get is saying, as Greenspan would later put it,[49] "Those of us who have looked to the self-interest of lending institutions to protect shareholders' equity (myself especially) are in a state of shocked disbelief." And you're still admired as a genius because that's so well put.

THE HABIT OF HOSTILITY
Another sign of extreme arrogance is when someone demonstrates blatant, undisguised hostility and disdain toward the average Jane and Joe. This tends to be a cultural thing. Sometimes it's hidden just beneath the surface, while at other moments it takes the form

of outright aggression. But however it's expressed, client-focused hostility is a well-recognized feature of the Wall Street cultural landscape. Mind you, I don't think the ability to slam customers behind their backs is exactly a prerequisite for the jobs at investment banks or on the trading floor, but it certainly seems to be part of a revered tradition. Certainly, I'd say most neophytes jump into the melee on Wall Street with a great deal of ambition. It's a competitive bunch, as noted. A certain warrior mentality prevails. But the progression toward hostility is probably the result of evolutionary adjustment to their day-to-day working environments.

In 1971, psychologist Philip Zimbardo, PhD, directed the famous Stanford Prison Experiment. A group of students was randomly divided into two groups designated as "prisoners" and "guards." Adding an element of realism to the experiment, the prisoners were referred to only by number, wore baggy clothing, and were subjected to random schedules and sensory deprivation. The experiment was to last fourteen days but was terminated in six days because of what was described as brutal and sadistic behavior by the guards. The tests showed that each group moved progressively further into their respective roles and away from their identities as students.

Wall Street rookies often transform over time into some version of the "Take no prisoners, win at all cost" stereotype. But it's not one-sided; customers have to accept the poor treatment. When they do, the situation devolves into an abysmal cycle of arrogance and mistreatment.

How does it come about? What is it about this environment that creates an attitude ranging from chip-on-the-shoulder resentment to rip-their-face-off hostility? The dog-eat-dog nature of the business is infectious, but that doesn't fully account for the fixation—among many traders—for chewing up and spitting out their investors as well as their competitors, friends, rivals, trusting clients, and backstabbing cohorts.

Fear is certainly a factor. Those whose sense of accomplishment is based on money-making power also have the most to lose if the spigot is turned off—and in the hothouse environment of many Wall Street firms, it feels like that can happen at any moment (can, and indeed, does). This tends to make people jumpy. Where fear is present, suspicion and anger are not far behind. When the veneer of authenticity is fragile, the fear of being discovered as a fraud abounds.

Another contributing factor is the working environment. For those working in organizations like Goldman Sachs, Bear Stearns, and the late, lamented Lehman Brothers, the company is their life. Nothing less than 100 percent devotion is required. There are no limits on the hours worked; around-the-clock availability is the norm. Day or night, whether at work, socializing, traveling, or vacationing—the company always comes first. Naturally, this accretion of obligations, total fealty to the ruling employer, engenders an excess of the pervasive "I Deserve It" attitude that gives every person making these sacrifices a monumental sense of entitlement. Such cultures also make and worship their self-created messiahs of profit.

But when such dedication is demanded, only some of the concomitant resentment can be directed toward the master corporation and its rulers. There is plenty of leftover fury to send in all directions: toward rivals; toward fellow employees; toward clients. And, ultimately, toward you and me.

What did we do that was wrong? The answer is pretty simple. As they see it, we gave them our money. We *allowed* ourselves to be duped. That showed our weakness, our stupidity, our blindness. They figured out how to go one better than us, put one over on us, and if we were fools enough to go along with it—so goes the rationale of hostility—then we deserve what's coming to us.

In some cultures, disparagement of the customer (sucker) is overt. In other firms the disdain is more gentlemanly and muted. But whether the anger is active or passive, it usually finds expression in words and actions. P. T. Barnum's resentment was eternalized by his famous quotation, "There's a sucker born every minute." You can almost hear the Wall Street choir singing "Hallelujah!"

The public tends to react with shock when confronted with the e-mails or private conversations between traders in which their disdain for the public is fully expressed. Congressional committee members had a field day with revelations of attitudinal crimes that were revealed by the private e-mails of Goldman Sachs super trader Fabrice Tourre. His first sin was referring to himself, with tongue firmly in cheek, as "Fabulous Fab"—a sobriquet that was instantly picked up in the media. But the deeper problems with his attitude came out in other ways. Referring to the already-gasping subprime market, in an e-mail to his girlfriend, Tourre declared that the business was "totally dead," saying, "[T]he poor little subprime borrowers will not last too long!!!" As his congressional questioners pointed out, while noting that the subprime market was collapsing, Tourre continued to promote the product, specifically mentioning (in June 2007) that he had managed to sell some of the toxic bonds to "widows and orphans" that he "ran into at the airport."[50]

They live through fear, greed, hostility, backstabbing and front stabbing, dark moments of utter fear, and triumphant periods of giddy victory. All of these experiences simply sharpen the claws.

These days, I meet many people who are amazed at the bonuses that Wall Street gave itself after so many companies had been bailed out by public funds (your dollars and mine), and after so many millions of investors had seen their retirement funds cut in half. For this service to our nation and economy, the masters of Wall Street arrogance paid themselves $18.4 billion in bonuses in 2009.[51] (At Christmastime there is a guy in New York who walks around and hands out $100 bills to random folks he selects to help. This bonus amount of $18.4 billion is enough to hand every man, woman, and child in the United States $61 each. Imagine what *that* would do for the economy!)

But the ridiculous size of those bonuses was no real surprise. I don't think it was really greed that dictated the proportion of the rewards. It certainly wasn't necessity. It was simply an expression of total indifference to public opinion. We, the public, didn't matter, even though we'd saved their companies. We were just the public. Those bonuses were just Wall Street's display of general hostility, translated into a single gesture: It was their middle finger, raised on high. Not surprisingly, I think we got the message.

THE PONZI-MADOFF "SCREW 'EM" PHILOSOPHY

During any era of runaway extreme arrogance, the Bernie Madoffs of the financial world have a special opportunity to flourish. It's important to acknowledge that no one who ever devised a Ponzi scheme could do it on his own. By its very nature, such a scheme requires the collaboration of numerous investors who believe they are getting something special, an insider's deal that sets them apart from all the less-fortunate, less-important people who are excluded from the special club that gives them privileges. It makes sense that every time one of these schemes unravels, it turns out that many of the investors were celebrities, or stars, or members of the higher echelons of social strata. This isn't surprising because people who expect or demand special attention have every reason to believe that they should also have special access to money-making opportunities. Nothing in their lives puts them among the "average," so why should their money be mixed in with the hoi polloi's? They want favors, and when there's a Bernie Madoff around, they get them.

Of course, we are all susceptible to a certain extent. Let's face it: We all want to belong to the club that won't have us as a member. When Groucho Marx delivered that line, he went to the core of human truth and identified one of our greatest vulnerabilities.

For many years, I tried to win the business of one of Madoff's clients. My prospect dismissed my queries by telling me that I was no Bernie Madoff, but because I was such a nice kid, he'd take me to lunch with Bernie so maybe I could learn something. I was furious. I missed my lunch with Bernie Madoff, and in retrospect, I'm sorry that I did. I wish I'd seen, firsthand, how he worked the magic. He created exactly the kind of club that Groucho was talking about, the one that wouldn't have you as a member. Too exclusive. Too many privileges. Costs too much to get in. And of course, because Bernie told every member, "Don't tell anyone," an extraordinary number of people wanted to join.

My generous prospect was wiped out by Bernie—the same one who had gotten me that invitation to lunch that I regretfully declined. He belonged; I didn't. At the time, he couldn't figure out why I didn't want to come along. And it was hard to argue with him. He had been with Bernie for thirty years. Thirty years! During that time, he had enjoyed the kinds of returns for which Madoff was famous—at least 12 percent a year, sometimes more— in a market that went through five full cycles of boom and bust, and boom again. (During one seven-year period, there were only three months when Madoff reported losses.)[52] How could I argue for "due diligence"? How much more diligent could he possibly be? My friend knew the track record of Bernie's firm, not just as an outside observer but as a participant, someone who had been there all along, who had realized real gains, and who had lived extremely well off his profits.

Well, what about auditing the books? Is that what my friend should have done?

It was unthinkable. Maybe a new guy, just coming into the club, could ask to audit the books. (It was later revealed that those who did ask for due diligence were denied—and some of them joined in anyway!) But over the years, my friend and Bernie had become very close. They were neighbors in Palm Beach. They had chateaus near each other in France. "If I had a crisis in my life, and I needed to reach out to someone, I would have reached out to Bernie," my friend told me. When you have a relationship like that, you don't turn around and ask to audit the books.

To someone on the outside, there was something surreal about the returns that Bernie was delivering. You look at a steady payout of 1 or 2 percent a month, during up cycles and down, and say to yourself, "There's something unbelievable about this." I wasn't the only one who was skeptical.

Harry Markopolos, the Boston investor who spent so many years trying to get the SEC to investigate Madoff, first learned of Bernie through a European investor. Rene-Thierry ("Thierry") Magon de la Villehuchet was a very rich and princely investor who ran a fund called Access[53] (a name that, all too ironically, expressed what people wanted from it). Originally, Markopolos was asked to look at Madoff's fund to discover what sort of formula Bernie was using that made it possible for him to show such reliable results, month after month, year after year. The graph of reported profits for Bernie's fund showed a 45-degree incline, with few bumps and no downslides. From his own experience as a professional investor, Markopolos realized this was a revenue stream "which simply doesn't exist in finance." After a few minutes' review of Bernie's reported results, Markopolos concluded, "There's no way this is real. This is bogus."[53]

Thierry, as it turned out, had made only the feeblest attempts to check the reported results against actual market performance, but the Frenchman had all the usual reasons for going with Madoff and for trusting him. Thierry referred to Madoff as his "partner," and it was only with the greatest reluctance that he finally revealed his partner's identity. ("I'm sorry—I'm not supposed to tell his name to anyone. If I do, he might not give me any capacity."[55]) Questioned further, Thierry admitted that the account he had opened with Madoff Securities permitted Bernie "to use the money any way he wants. I've given him full discretion to put my clients' money with his personal money when it's needed."[55] Thierry felt absolutely confident, without checking, that the money was being invested wisely. First of all, he had the on-paper report graphing that impressive 45-degree angle. Second, as Thierry declared, "It's secured by his good name."

When Markopolos looked at the "strategy" that Bernie was allegedly using (a "split-strike" conversion) and ran the numbers, he quickly concluded that Madoff would have to get in and out of the market at exactly the right times—over and over and over again—to get such mind-bending results.[57] A split-strike conversion could "bracket" an investment—limiting potential profit when the market went up and guarding against big losses if the market tanked—but it was impossible to get the kind of month-after-month results that Bernie was getting with that kind of strategy. Furthermore, as Markopolos began to comprehend the scope of Bernie's investments, he concluded that Bernie would have to be doing such an enormous number of trades that they would definitely show up in the market. Looking at historical results, there was no indication of Bernie's market activity.

"Bernie Madoff was a fraud," Markopolos concluded. "And whatever he was actually doing, it was enough to put him in prison. . . ."[58] Madoff had not registered with the SEC as an investment advisory firm or a hedge fund, so he wasn't regulated. He was simply a guy you gave your money to, to do whatever he wanted to do with it, and in return he handed you a nice profit. He was the Wizard of Oz, and he made everybody so happy that they didn't want to look behind the curtain."[59]

Of course, Markopolos was not the only one with doubts. As he began to ask around, Markopolos realized that many Wall Street insiders assumed Bernie was doing something illegal.[60] The only question was, *How?* According to one theory, he was "front-running." Bernie's other business was as a broker-dealer, which meant he had access to market information that gave him prior knowledge indicating when certain securities would move up or down. Taking advantage of that information is commonly known as insider trading. It broke the law. But so what? If it accounted for Bernie's inconceivably consistent returns, it was one possible explanation.[61]

Another theory held that Bernie was using his hedge fund to borrow from investors. To Markopolos, this appeared ludicrous. It would mean that Madoff was somehow making more than 12 to 15 percent annually, using the money he borrowed from investors, which was beyond credibility. The only possibility, Markopolos concluded, was that Bernie was running a massive Ponzi scheme—constantly raising enough funds from one set of investors to pay off others while he created a trail of paper profits that he duly reported in very official-looking documents (providing reports that were neither audited nor verified by anyone outside his close inner circle). Markopolos realized that the level of fraud was enormous.

The fact is, extreme arrogance entraps not only the innocent and the foolhardy, but also those who are equally arrogant. For Bernie to succeed, he needed feeder funds like the one provided by the overly trusting Thierry de la Villehuchet. He needed huge numbers of people who would suspend their disbelief and put their trust in someone who held some secret formula that defied all mathematical probability. He needed people who gave him full authority to make their wealth grow without making the slightest effort to determine how their money was being used. He needed a great number of people who considered themselves extremely deserving, uniquely qualified, and remarkably privileged—in other words, far, far above average.

He found them, and they found him. It was a marriage of convenience that ended tragically. Thierry de la Villehuchet, the French fund manager who had held absolute faith in Bernie, committed suicide, leaving notes of apology to his wife and business associates. (Thierry's fund, Access International, lost about $1.4

billion of his clients' money—including investments from many of the royal families of Europe—and he and his business partner lost a personal fortune worth $55 million.[62]) And then, on December 11, 2010, Bernie's son Mark David Madoff—his reputation irreparably damaged by association with his father's name and firm, faced with numerous lawsuits from investors, dogged by constant media scrutiny—committed suicide in his Manhattan apartment.

Naturally, after some reflection over the pain wrought and lives ruined, Bernie apologized. Right? Didn't he? Even Frank Sinatra sang, "Regrets, I've had a few."

Wrong. Not Bernie! He didn't give a damn.

Early in 2010, reports of Bernie's attitude had begun to emerge from the federal correctional complex in Butner, North Carolina. Prodded by another inmate who wanted to know how Bernie felt about divesting investors of some $65 billion, the former fund manager reportedly replied, "Fuck my victims. I carried them for twenty years, and now I'm doing 150 years."[63]

Like I say, I do believe Bernie Madoff is one of the worst human beings imaginable. But he couldn't have done what he did without a lot of help from those who handed their money over to him.

All the more reason—if any were needed—to keep a close eye on our Arrogance Index.

Chapter 4

THEY ARE IN OUR MIDST

Form Trumps Substance

Among mere mortals, there are many of us who feel that we are in some way responsible for our actions. And, at least in theory, the laws of the land suggest that's the way we're supposed to feel. The gentleman who comes into a bank, holds up the teller at gunpoint, and demands everything in the drawer is generally regarded as a thief. He's personally charged with the commission of a crime, he's arrested, tried, thrown in jail, does time. He's somehow held accountable for what he did. He may argue that he was nuts at the time, but he can't maintain that *someone else* walked into that bank—some kind of zombie who might or might not have been him. He may say that someone made him do it, or he felt compelled to do it because of poverty, desperation, or whatever. But still, he's the guy. It's all on him.

What many people don't realize—or try not to realize—is that in the fast-paced world of esoteric investments and corporate decision-making, caught up in the rising tide of arrogance, the objective is to maximize personal profit and minimize personal responsibility. In a climate of total arrogance, everyone is aiming toward a single goal—profitability—and the ingenuity of everyone involved is directed toward achieving that goal. We've seen how this plays out in investment banks. The individual trader wants to make a killing, personally, so he or she will get the fat bonus. The group wants to prove that it can outmatch any other group in the bank in terms of ingenuity, clout, and daring. (And they can be pretty certain that as long as they are the profit champs, they'll have the fewest restraints, oversights, and limits on their trades.) And the banks—well, if we're talking about the very big ones, for the most part they are managed by people the size of whose egos is exceeded only by the size of their incomes, individuals who have clawed their way to the top and do not easily let go of all they have acquired.

But what about *risk*—the great leveler? If all these guys playing poker are intent on beating each other, and the stakes are getting higher and higher, isn't there some point at which some of them are going to have to cash in their chips and say, "That's it—can't go any higher. I'm out"? That's how it used to be among bankers because there were house rules. You couldn't take depositors' money and gamble it in the stock market. But that rule became an antique in 1999[64] when the Glass-Steagall Act was nullified by Congress and banks were allowed to gamble thirty or forty times what they had in their vaults. What was the upper limit of leverage? There was none. Oh, sure, there was a level at which people within the bank began muttering, "We're too leveraged," or "Too much risk," but then they looked over the fence at another bank that had even more risk than theirs, and they didn't worry quite so much.

When Bear Stearns went under, it was leveraged to the tune of nearly 44 to 1.[65] (That's a probable figure; even the bank officers weren't sure exactly how much it was leveraged.) That means that one chip was in reserve for every forty-four chips on the table. And who was responsible for settling up? Think about leveraging yourself forty-four times. Take all of your cash, stocks, and home equity, and borrow forty-four times that amount. If you have $250,000 equity in your home, $200,000 in retirement accounts, and $50,000 in checking and savings accounts, *you would have to borrow $22,000,000!* If you managed to earn just 5 percent on your money, you'd add a cool $1,100,000 and triple your net worth!

Who was responsible? No one, apparently. In the tortuous weekend when Bear Stearns ran out of money—during the fourteen months when its share price fell from \$172.69 to \$2.00,[66] and when the only hope for survival was a rescue deal with J.P. Morgan—what were the officers and directors of Bear most worried about?

Indemnity. Freedom from responsibility.

They wanted no liability. They wanted protection from lawsuits. If the bank was going to merge, they wanted personal assurances that their private assets would not be tampered with. They dug in their heels. Without indemnity, no merger deal. They'd rather see the entire company go bust than take any personal responsibility for what they had done—individually and collectively—to shipwreck the company. And so, they got what they wanted. As William D. Cohan writes in *House of Cards: A Tale of Hubris and Wretched Excess on Wall Street*, "According to the terms of the merger agreement, J.P. Morgan agreed to 'indemnify and hold harmless' each current and former Bear director and officer 'from liability for matters arising at or prior to the completion of the merger' as well as keeping in place Bear Stearns's existing indemnification agreements 'for six years following completion of the merger.'"[67]

A hunger for and belief in indemnification are two of the salient characteristics of the arrogant. They presume the entitlement of being beyond reproach, and even above questioning. Alas, there have been many examples of this behavior in recent history—not just on Wall Street, but also on the highways and byways of corporate America.

ARROGANCE THE ENRON WAY

Within the bowels of Enron, back at the turn of the twenty-first century when it still existed as a much-envied company, there was an annual ritual loved by reigning royalty like chief operating officer Jeffrey Skilling and chief financial officer Andrew Fastow. It went like this: You set up cardholders, creating five different categories numbered one through five. Number one is for top-ranking individuals. Number five is for those at the low end of the totem pole. Then, on separate cards, you write the name of each employee who is to be evaluated. Now let the revels begin.

If you're a manager, the idea is to play this game (with lives, careers, incomes, egos) in such a way so as to obtain the best possible performance rating for the people who report to you. The employees who end up in slots one or two are going to get the biggest bonuses and raises, so naturally, the number of people you can recommend for those ratings is limited. Before each of these big annual meetings, some horse trading went on as managers agreed they would give a little here (sacrificing one person) and take a little there (on behalf of another). Then, as the big day began, each manager made a case for the employees who were going to end up in those top one or two spots, while others were shuffled off to positions three, four, five. On those performance-review days at Enron, debates could get pretty fierce, but by the end of the day, everyone knew where they stood in the pecking order. Each manager's performance, and the performance of those who reported to them, had been duly judged by their peers and either found wanting or worthy. Bonuses and promotions were doled out accordingly.

In broad strokes, this was not much different from the kind of annual performance evaluation that goes on within any company. What made the process distinctive—the thing that was so uniquely Enronian—was the observable level of vicious competitiveness in these meetings. The entire year's work of a conscientious employee could be swept aside in an instant if Fastow or Skilling wanted to make room for one of their guys who had bent the truth or broken the rules to achieve stellar on-paper results for a risky and ill-considered venture. By the end of one of these sessions, everyone knew who was being rewarded and who was being punished. Those who played along with the harebrained and self-serving schemes of Fastow and Skilling got the highest performances ratings—they were the ones and twos. The rest were labeled drudges. They did their jobs, perhaps, fulfilled their roles, but when their performance was evaluated at Enron, they were numbered among the deadheads. They were the threes, fours, and fives. It was the perfect system for rewarding arrogance.

And the system worked. The arrogant rose to the top, and stayed there. These were the faithful followers of situational ethics and momentary morality—until, of course, the whole company collapsed ignominiously into an ash heap of damaged prospects and ruined careers.

Against such a pervasive system of arrogance-reward, voices calling for restraint were but distant cries in the wilderness. Eventually, even CEO Kenneth Lay became concerned that the efforts of his brash crew of hard-driving entrepreneurial geniuses might be getting a little out of hand. His palliative, rather than change a system that so clearly rewarded ballsy boldness and blood-and-guts internal warfare, was to bring in an outside speaker who could chasten the troops and warn them against the dangers of unbridled greed. The chosen speaker? None other than former junk bond king, Wall Street titan, and felon, Michael Milken.

Their rationale, of course, was the same as inviting a former crackhead to warn high school kids about the dangers of doing drugs. And when it came to doing the stuff and making the deals, Milken was indeed a prime example of arrogant wrongheadedness—a living, breathing illustration of what can go awry when you place yourself above all others. In the 1980s, as head of Drexel Burnham's high-yield bond-trading department, Milken ran an operation that had a 100 percent return on investment.[68] As the sale of junk bonds gained momentum and his arrogance grew to match the size of his reported profits, he discovered that he could create partnerships that benefited not only his department but also some close associates, money managers, and his own children—all at the expense of the funds he was supposed to be managing.[69] At the time, he either failed to notice that he was violating a number of SEC rules (not to mention some fairly basic standards of propriety), or, more likely, simply thought he could get away with it. And, actually, he did get away with such things—at least until 1990, when he pleaded guilty to six counts of securities and tax violations, agreeing, in the end, to pay $200 million in fines, along with $900 million to investors (Drexel's and others identified by the SEC) who had been hurt by his actions. After that, he headed off for a couple of years in jail.[70]

Now, having served jail time and having reconsidered his youthful folly, Milken had become a regular on the lecture circuit. Lay introduced Milken as an old hand who "has had the experience of growing a very, very successful finance-trading organization." Lay added: "I thought there were some things we could learn from Mike as to his experiences at Drexel, both from the good times and the bad."[71]

Indeed, Milken had a good spiel to deliver: about the way success could breed carelessness; about liberal interpretation of accounting rules; and about the risks of getting caught.[71] His audience, which included most of the upper management from Enron (Fastow, unfortunately, was in London doing a deal and unable to attend[73]), listened with rapt attention. Indeed, they could not do otherwise, since this instructional meeting had been called by their CEO, and attendance was pretty much mandatory. But after it was all over, according to *New York Times* reporter Kurt Eichenwald, the Enron personnel retreated one and all to the nearest bar, where they had the opportunity to shake their heads, laugh, and wonder aloud: "What was *that* all about?"[74]

Well, their CEO had tried, but it was already too late. By then, Fastow had already become adept at playing a dual role as CFO of Enron and manager of "special-purpose entities,"[75] with which Enron supposedly had "arm's-length" dealings. From these entities—with names like LJM, Raptor, JEDI, and Chewco—he and some select insiders would reap $161 million in personal rewards from their investment of $161,000.[76] By then, the managers of Enron had so intimidated the conscientious accountants (and would-be whistleblowers) within Arthur Andersen that everyone realized all the usual rules regarding reporting of profits and conflict-of-interest were out the window. By then, Lay had already given many nods of approval to the activities of Fastow and Skilling as they acquired unrelated businesses for millions more than they were worth, setting up shell companies to help Enron report profits and hide losses. By then, analysts at Enron's investment banks (like Merrill Lynch[77]) had discovered that they would be fired or demoted if they gave less-than-stellar ratings to Enron stock. By then, the board of Enron had okayed the impossibly peculiar and highly improper accommodation that allowed Fastow to act as CFO of Enron while, at the same time, serving as a principal in the outside funds with which Enron was doing business.

All that was water under the bridge. And as that water passed by, there stood Kenneth Lay, with Michael Milken by his side, warning all these kids that they might be polluting their own playground. Of course the kids didn't listen. Why should they? Lay and the board had signed off on all the deals and had constantly pumped fuel into a culture where arrogance was rewarded, diligence was derided, and only those who could stomach delusion and evasion would survive the rigors of trench warfare. If you wanted your name to go in the number-one slot at performance-review time, you didn't heed the warnings of a fallen Milken. You responded to the coercion of a rising Fastow.

THE WORLDCOM VIEW: BIGNESS IS ALL

Results, results, results. That's all Bernie Ebbers at WorldCom ever asked for. As for the details, he always admitted there was a lot he didn't know, and couldn't know; it was all much too complicated for him. He was a busy guy who wasn't good at reading the fine print, and, besides—how is someone with a multibillion-dollar company that's growing by leaps and bounds supposed to keep track of what everyone on his staff is doing? Bernie didn't know and couldn't know. He was innocent. Just ask him.

The problem, as we now know, was the way WorldCom fizzed and sizzled and popped during the run-up on telecom stocks. Between 1991 and 1997, the height of the acquisition years, WorldCom, with charismatic Bernie Ebbers at its head, went on an acquisition spree, snapping up more than sixty-five companies. The cost of these acquisitions was about $60 billion, and the company accumulated some $41 billion in debt.[78] Happiness is a soaring stock price, and during those years, Bernie and WorldCom did everything in their power to keep investors satisfied with results. The ticker speaks for itself. Starting out as pennies-per-share, by 1997 WorldCom's ever-rosier reports and forecasts captured an ever-widening swath of investors who pushed the price over $60 per share.[79]

Unfortunately, it's impossible to get into the intracranial lobes of Ebbers and ask him, *What were you thinking?* Nor is it quite possible to reconstruct the motives and motivations of those who reported to him and were riding on the bandwagon. But it is possible to reconstruct those heady days of runaway arrogance by reading court testimony, along with the account of Cynthia Cooper, the internal auditor who blew the whistle on the whole thing. According to Bernie and his crew, it was all our fault.

By *our fault*, I mean the public at large. Stockholders in his company. Journalists who fell over themselves praising WorldCom and lauding its immense growth. The many analysts who failed to analyze, the regulators who failed to regulate, and even those who were left out of the entire fizzy, exciting game but admired or envied those who had the prescience to get in early and ride to the top of the Ferris wheel. For a while, it looked like Bernie had all of "us" behind him.

The first thing we did was get him all excited about a business model that was based on steady, inexorable growth. When WorldCom acquired MFS Communications and MCI Communications, giving them an edge in international as well as local and regional telecom transmission, we sent Bernie a message that said, "This is really exciting—keep it up!" In addition to pushing his stock price up, we ogled the feats of WorldCom on all the major business shows, where the stimulating news of runaway success was absorbed by hundreds of millions of viewers. America was treated to the come-from-behind, up-from-nowhere story of an enterprising young man who was on his way to glory. If the humble youth, Bernie Ebbers, acquired just a touch of arrogance at that point—if he started to believe his own press—can you blame him?

It's no wonder that Bernie hired some really smart guys who could keep up appearances when growth slowed or demand fell— when the moving parts failed to mesh, or the whole agglomeration of telecom-related concerns began to look like a screwball mess. For the purposes of keeping up appearances, none, it turned out, was more talented than CFO Scott "Smoke and Mirrors" Sullivan. Talented? Wait—no—he was amazing. Paving the way for men like Fastow at Enron, Sullivan at WorldCom became adept at inventing shell companies that could help out the balance sheet by producing on-paper revenue for WorldCom that would show up on the books at convenient times of the year—just before reports were issued to shareholders. He could turn operating expenses into capital expenditures, which helped enormously in reporting to the IRS, because the costs could be amortized far into the future. Best of all, he could get everyone working together on this—WorldCom's lawyers, the accounting firms, employees, and a whole slew of investment banks eager to do business with an ever-more-muscular Goliath of enterprise.

To do all this, Bernie and Scott had many operational tools. They could get all their main guys in a room and raise some concerns about stock prices, tell them to do something about it, and all those guys would leave the room and start to work on projects that would, indeed, improve the appearance of the annual report. As with the powerhouse team at Enron, the movers and shakers at WorldCom could come face-to-face with the true math and turn to the lowly accountant or bean counter and say, "That can't be right. Go back and fix it." With a frown or a laugh or a quick phone call, they could send the message that, "Your answer to this question (or your approval of this project) is directly related to the size of your end-of-the-year bonus." And for those who continued to believe in the math, recite the rules of proper accounting, or send up warnings of legal obstacles, Ebbers and Sullivan were quite good at sending a message of, "You know, you might *not* be a good fit with WorldCom right now," or "Let's have a little more cooperation here." Subtle tools, like sledgehammers, which sent shivers down the spines of those who felt some imperative—whether moral or conscientious—to say, "This emperor has no clothes."

Indeed, the emperor did have some clothes, but they were becoming progressively more threadbare, worn, and tattered. What Ebbers and Sullivan couldn't reveal to the public (us) is that WorldCom was hugely overextended, and that the many acquired companies—far from being smoothly integrated—resulted in redundant operations and inefficiencies that could not be overcome by Rube Goldberg improvisations. As the whole telecom industry moved into another phase, where the market was glutted with competitive services and costs ran way ahead of revenues, the WorldCom balance sheet began to look more and more like a work of fiction and less and less like the homework we tried to turn in for math class. When Cynthia Cooper blew the whistle, in 2000, the balance sheet was $2 billion out of whack. Back then, that was a big number—so big, in fact, that the WorldCom scam earned headlines as the largest accounting fraud in U.S. history.[80] (Minor league stuff today, sure, but back then it was big news.)

And it wasn't their fault. They weren't responsible.

How do we know?

Just ask Bernie Ebbers. As he told the court, he was never much good at accounting. He basically just looked over the documents and signed them. It was Scott Sullivan who should be blamed—the CFO who cooked the books. But Sullivan, in his testimony, said he understood from Bernie that he (Scott) was supposed to do anything to hit the numbers needed to support the stock price. Scott admitted to fraud in 2000, 2001, and 2002, but said he did it on Bernie's orders.

Sounds like a lot of finger pointing, doesn't it?

You know, come to think of it, to make it all work, Bernie and Scott really did need the cooperation of a lot of folks. Not bad folks, either; many of them just wanted to keep their jobs. Many were looking out for their families; they had bills to pay or mouths to feed. Many of them feared the consequences (quite justifiably) if they spoke out of turn or dug in their heels. Not cowards. Not thieves. Not mean. Folks, in a lot of ways, like you and me. Caught up in the Arrogance Cycle.

To be fair, some were also naive. Decent people are often at a loss to comprehend the egregiously bad among us. They can't imagine fraud beyond a certain scale—at least, not back then.

AIG AND THE DEMISE OF MORAL HAZARD

One way to put a cap on an arrogance gusher is with a disciplinary cap called conscience and morality. In the old days, moral hazard was the policeman on the block. It was the risk you ran of being punished for rash actions.

If you're a gambler and you borrow from the Mob to feed your habit, and you don't pay the guys back, the consequences are pretty clear: You're either going to get roughed up or snuffed. In civilized company, the repercussions for bad behavior are similar, but a lot more subtle. Run up a lot of debt on your credit cards, and the consequence is a shutdown of further credit, plus some long-standing damage to your credit rating. Fail to meet your mortgage payments, and the consequence is foreclosure. And so it goes. Businesses that go belly-up suffer the punishment of loss of income, loss of investor confidence, loss of credibility—not exactly the equivalent of a snuff-out, but still, in today's society, pretty serious. Morality is basically the old disciplinary rules of home and classroom, writ large: If you break the rules, buddy, *the piper will be paid!*

But that was in the old days. More recently, some paradigms of arrogance have discovered that the system can work differently. You might suffer some consequences—say, a lot of bad press—but as for true consequence, well, the landscape has changed. True consequence is so yesterday. If you have a sufficient amount of arrogance, here's what you can do: You can shift it to moral hazard.

First, you offer to sell insurance to a lot of people who tell you that they need it and are willing to pay for it. You guarantee all these people that under your insurance policy, if they have losses, you will repay them with full compensation. Such insurance policies are in demand, so your business grows, until you have several hundred protégés who are highly motivated to sell huge amounts of this insurance. And each one of those employees becomes intensely focused and motivated as they realize their compensation will increase enormously if they stick with the plan and sell lots more insurance. They will all become multimillionaires.

Of course, as the business grows, you realize you could potentially owe a lot of people a lot of money on those policies. And if you were a real insurance company abiding by the usual rules, that would mean that you would have to hold enough in reserve and in reinsurance to protect against the risk of losses. But here's where you've done something exceptionally clever. Even though you are providing insurance, you have set yourself up as an investment bank, free from the usual guidelines and restrictions that would apply to an insurer. In fact, despite all the guarantees that you have provided to the people you have insured, you don't need to hold *any* reserves. That's right. Zero. Zilch. Nada. You collect fees for insuring them, you provide them with promises to repay in the case of losses, but you don't need to hold anything in reserve to *pay* for those losses, should they occur.

And now comes the best part of all. Sure enough, eventually there are some losses on those properties that you've insured, and, as is their right, those people holding the insurance come to you looking for payments. But there's no way you can meet those payments because you presupposed this would never happen. So you turn to a few friends who are in the government, and you ask for taxpayer money to pay back the people you've insured. Your friends bitch and moan a little, but they'd hate to see you go bust, so, sure enough, they give you taxpayer money to pay off the claims against you. And you're done.

Sweet.

And where's the true consequence? There is none. No penalty for you. Some bad press, sure; what else did you expect? But that's about it.

Hard to believe?

Moral hazard is the absence of blame or consequence for the perpetrator. Consequence and liability are shifted from the guilty to the unsuspecting innocent.

Joseph Cassano of AIG pulled it off beautifully. In fact, when it was all over, his only regret was that he couldn't stay around to clean up the mess. According to Joe, if everyone had just put a little more faith in him, he could have made it all come out right.

How's that for arrogance?

But . . . as always . . . he couldn't have done it alone.

Cassano, who had previously worked at Drexel Burnham in the junk bond days of Michael Milken, joined American International Group (AIG) in 1987, where he was made chief financial officer of the newly formed Financial Products Division. In 1994 he was promoted to head of the Transaction Development Group, and by 1998, he was dealing heavily in credit default swaps on collateralized debt obligations. Basically, his division was an insurance company, guaranteeing to other banks that tranches of securities backed by home loans would be insured against losses. By 2008 AIG Financial Products Division had insured $441 billion of securities, of which $57.8 billion were structured debt securities backed by subprime loans.[81]

The relatively small division—.325 percent of the employees in a company that employed 116,000—began to account for an ever-larger share of revenues.[82] In 1999 Cassano's group produced 4.2 percent of overall operating income for AIG; by 2005 that figure had increased more than four times, to 17.5 percent. And the members of the unit did extremely well. Between 2001 and 2008, the Financial Products Division paid out $3.56 billion to its fewer than 400 employees.[83]

In September of 2008, the ratings agencies finally awakened to the fact that AIG was in way over its head. As increasing numbers of homeowners with subprime loans found themselves unable to meet higher payments or refinance their mortgages, as foreclosure rates soared and the value of CDOs crumbled, AIG's credit rating was downgraded. What followed was a liquidity crisis that sent tremors through the market. The investment banks that had CDOs "insured" by AIG—most notably, Goldman Sachs—began to pressure the insurer to meet the payments that had been promised. No way. Either AIG was going to go under or . . .

This is where the federal government stepped in, providing some $85 billion of guaranteed taxpayer money to avoid the collapse of the insurance giant.[84] Remember that moment?

If Cassano is to be believed, none of his unit's activities were underhanded. Or even secretive. In his prepared testimony for the Congressional Financial Crisis Inquiry Commission on June 30, 2010, he declared, "I was truthful at all times about the unrealized accounting losses and did my very best to estimate them accurately, in consultation with others at AIG-FP, as well as with my supervisors, AIG's senior accounting staff, and its internal and external auditors."[85]

In his testimony, Cassano went on to say:

The first stage in the approval process was internal at AIG-FP. Every proposed CDS transaction first was reviewed by an experienced AIG-FP credit officer, who performed an independent analysis of the proposed deal. The credit officer analyzed the trade fundamentals, the proposed terms and conditions, and the asset classes.

After that initial review, University of Pennsylvania [sic] Professor Gary Gorton, who served as a consultant to AIG-FP, worked with our experienced analysts to refine the deal structure. To complete this review, Professor Gorton used a sophisticated actuarial model to make sure the proposed deal was fundamentally sound and to determine an appropriate attachment point. This process was designed to minimize risk to AIG-FP.

As for Professor Gorton, his views on "The Panic of 2007" are encapsulated in a paper on the subject prepared for the Federal Reserve Bank of Kansas City, Jackson Hole Conference, in August 2008.[86] Explaining how all the confusion occurred, Professor Gorton (a professor at Yale, *not* the University of Pennsylvania) suggested that "This nesting or interlinking of securities, structures, and derivatives resulted in a loss of information and ultimately in a loss of confidence since, as a practical matter, looking through to the underlying mortgages and modeling the different levels of structure was not possible."[87] Clearly, such complex structures led to problems. As Professor Gorton says, "When house prices began to slow their growth and ultimately fall, the bubble bursting, the value of the chain of securities began to decrease. But, exactly which securities were affected? And, where were these securities? What was the expected loss? Even today we do not know the answers to these questions."

So, the former consultant to AIG-FP chalked up the crisis to a failure of information flow. That's one theory. More likely, I think, the underlying cause was the arrogance factor.

And who was culpable? Who had to bear the consequences? Certainly not Joseph Cassano. After a two-year investigation, the Justice Department could find no evidence of wrongdoing on his part. All charges were dropped.[88] Joe walked away with his earnings while you and I picked up the tab.

Does that piss you off as much as it does me?

CHAPTER 5

REALITY DETACHMENT

Loose the Chains!

What does it feel like to get caught up in an Arrogance Cycle? Why is it so hard to see what's going on and somehow resist the mania? Why are the temptations so great?

Optimism is a magnet. Who among us would not like to believe that tomorrow will be better than today—that we have the potential to be richer, more powerful, happier, and more content? It's written into the human DNA. Unfortunately, the ingredients of optimism are too often the same ingredients that go into arrogance, and they're largely driven by the subtleties of hope and a desire for certainty.

As we can see from some of the historical examples of boom and bust, every cycle has played to this fundamental human need or desire. We want things to get better. We tend to follow those who hold out the promise that tomorrow will not, in fact, drift in this petty pace from day to day, but will, instead, bring in the gravy train. I'm sure there are cultures where people have developed a certain immunity to the promises of greater wealth or a more lavish lifestyle, but that's certainly not the case around here.

Unbridled optimism is the core principle upon which our nation was founded, and it continues to be the driving force behind so much of what we do and who we are. Think of Columbus's insanely optimistic journey. Wanting to open new trade routes and load up on gold and spices, he set off blindly into a region thought to be filled with sea monsters and other perils. Hard on his heels came waves upon waves of immigrants, pursuing the promise of far more earthly goods and heavenly rewards in the New World than they ever could have found in the Old. Dyed-in-the-wool optimists set out in carts, wagons, rafts, and riverboats, pushing westward toward lands that they firmly believed were made for you and me. And their tradition is sustained today by every immigrant who takes a low-paying job in the belief that he or she will ultimately find prosperity, by every entrepreneur who starts a bootstrap enterprise with sweat equity and chump change, by every young college graduate who takes on tons of debt in order to get an advanced degree promising professional advancement and perpetual employment, and by every young turk who invests personal or public money in great enterprises and hopes for the best.

But it's not just Americans who are wishers and wanderers. History books are filled with the achievements of optimists. Forgotten, or neglected, are the dire warnings of stick-in-the-muds. Without the doers and dreamers, where would we be? Our hearts beat faster when we witness the achievements of an individual, a team, or a company that comes from behind and beats the odds. We want to run up Philadelphia's famous steps with Rocky Balboa and defeat Apollo Creed as the whole world watches in awe. Optimism is in our bones. Positive messages travel fast, whether by word of mouth, in print, through silicon chips, or on pop-up screens. This is what we're all about. Whether we're on the playing field, in the boardroom, or out on the dance floor, the whole idea is that we're supposed to come from behind (or come from nowhere!) and seize the day.

The second important characteristic of an Arrogance Cycle is runaway excess. Ever since pharaohs built pyramids to house their remains and Greeks constructed temples to honor their gods, we have shown a remarkable amount of tolerance for those who espouse grandiose schemes of human advancement, and for those who go on to incur huge cost overruns in their building projects. We seem to have an insatiable yearning for monuments of all kinds—sports stadia, vaulted houses of worship, or soaring skyscrapers bearing corporate signatures. We tend to adore kings, queens, royalty, and superstars, and we grant them the *rights* to excess as rapidly as they can cook up the next big project or design profligate ways to display wealth or indulge fantasies. We love it. We ogle Michael Jackson's pseudomagical kingdom, the palace that Helmsley built, the many towers of Trump. Tour buses in Beverly Hills are filled to capacity. We visit the magisterial summer palaces at Newport with their temple-like ballrooms, their imported marble, all the finery from a Gatsby era when Old World craftspeople were employed to create New World excess. We have Rockefeller estates, Carnegie mansions, Hearst castles, where our eyes glaze over and we catch our breath trying to imagine mere humans—people like you and me—occupying such surreal spaces.

True, every once in a while, during the course of history, some democratic or revolutionary movement bellows its objections to such lavish spending, the self-indulgent lifestyles and ostentatious displays. Occasionally, we do get ticked off at kings and queens, tsars and tsarinas, money barons and baronesses. "Too much! That's it! Your fun is over!" Things may get nasty for a while. What's remarkable, however, is how the exemplars of excess always return to claim their rights, lavish up their home decor, and set off on spending sprees the likes of which (we always declare) we've never seen before.

Taken together, the signs of surging optimism, accompanied by the signals of runaway excess, are sure indicators of an upward curve in the Arrogance Cycle. I realize it's bad luck to speak ill of optimists, but we must acknowledge that they do tend to drift sharply away from reality. Although we wouldn't be where we are today if we didn't have the staunch visionaries who believed all things are possible, the trouble is, a great optimist can also be a great liar. Whether the pejorative applies or not usually depends on outcomes. "If we put our resources and energy and creative powers into building this company, it can happen" is a good example of the positive use to which optimism can be put. "We're too big to fail, we can get out of any mess, and we're smarter than the rest of the guys," is also a pretty good example of optimism, but unfortunately, an out-and-out lie. And it's also a key indicator of arrogance.

One challenge, for those of us who would like to be alerted to the rise of the Arrogance Cycle, is to distinguish one kind of optimism from another. When are optimistic projections, forecasts, and assumptions still in the range of reality? And when do they constitute out-and-out lies? Moreover, is the liar smart enough to recognize when he's totally full of it? If we're going to get any reliable measurement of arrogance, we need to figure out some kind of measurement for what's possible and what isn't. Otherwise, we'll be perpetually mixing up delusion with vision, and we'll end up believing that rosy predictions are as good as educated guesses. (They're not, and there's a big difference.)

Another challenge is trying to figure out when signals of excess are pointing to the onset of another Arrogance Cycle. If corporate jets are necessary for some executives, then how many are too many? If luxuries like vacation resorts and diamonds and high fashion are available to millions of us, how do we recognize when these splendors tip over into excess and decide we're spending too much on these things? Is a new Rolls-Royce a sign of excess or the satisfying fulfillment of an achievable and affordable luxury? Who is prepared to tell sports stars or media stars or the heads of multibillion-dollar companies that they have enough cars, houses, and perks? If this is the way people pursue happiness, they need to exercise the right to go for it. But when these excesses mount up, perhaps—just perhaps—it's some kind of signal that another Arrogance Cycle is upon us.

In 1997, I met with a seventeen-year-old Olympic gold medalist. He had won several golds in previous winter games. He was thirty minutes late for our meeting, and when he arrived by limousine, he had an exotic young lady on his rather large arm. He had just been signed to a total of $1 million in endorsement contracts for the next twelve months. He nonchalantly told me he was late because his car had passed a shop with a "cool" shirt in the window, and he'd had the driver circle back so he could buy the shirt. He boasted that it cost $160. He added that he could afford "this sort of crapola now." In spite of his adolescent hubris, there was something quite charming about him. He had a wonderful smile, and the television cameras and commentators liked him.

I talked about preserving the wealth he was receiving, and he said, "There's going to be a lot more where that came from. I'm going to really kick ass next time, and then there will be a lot more endorsements."

Gently (I thought), I explained that many of my clients earned over a million dollars a year and that they did not rent limos. I encouraged prudence and thrift, and talked about those classic famous athletes who flamed out financially and were left depressed and broke once their physical prowess and bank accounts had dwindled. I encouraged a savings plan and self-restraint.

Needless to say, I might as well have been talking to myself. It wasn't long before his eyes began to glaze over and he responded to the insistent buzz of his cell phone. By then, I already knew we weren't going to be a good match. His scenario would have to be played out on his own terms, and all I could do was wish him continued health, prowess, and good luck. Following his current investment plan—which was obviously no plan at all—I figured he would need all three. There wasn't anything I could do to help him. He continued to star in the next two series of Olympic Games and won quite a few more gold medals. Given his spending, I'd say that he was very fortunate. I hope he has become more financially responsible.

Invariably, unfettered optimism and excess do show up in the market. They are called bubbles, and they have occurred throughout history. In every case, there were signs of arrogance that accompanied the onset of the bubble. And, in every case, the damage wrought by arrogance was grim.

WHO WILL BUY THIS WONDERFUL TULIP?

One of the gaudiest and most notorious bubbles was the so-called Tulipomania in seventeenth-century Holland, when speculators began buying up certain tulips that had rare and delicate colorations. (Much later, botanists would discover that these rarities were created by certain viruses that thrived on the petals of the tulips, creating vivid streaks that only lasted for one generation.) The mania for trading tulips got launched in the early 1630s[89] when some noble families in Holland (who could afford it) began running up the prices by offering crazy sums for selected rarities. Before long, the forces of envy took over. Merchants, seeing a golden opportunity, joined in the bidding. This became a club with a select few members, so before long, everyone wanted in—whether they could afford it or not—and speculators of all classes and persuasions began buying on credit. When the bubble burst in 1637,[90] tulips that were selling for 6,000 guilders or more were essentially worthless, speculators were ruined, and Dutch society entered a slough of despond from which it was not to recover for several years.

As an example of hard cash and easy credit being risked on evanescent goods, Tulipomania is hard to beat. To anyone browsing through a Burpee or Wildflower Farms catalog, it's hard to imagine that a common garden flower could attain value equal to prime real estate in Amsterdam or Haarlem.

There are many reasons why a fervor of tulip speculation that occurred in Holland in the 1630s is just as relevant (and instructive!) as the mightier bubbles that we've seen in the past couple of decades. Though the initial enthusiasm for certain, select kinds of bulbs was started by well-informed importers, growers, and breeders, the market took on a carnival-like atmosphere. It was a market in which anyone could come and play. As Edward Chancellor recounts in his wonderful history of financial speculation (with the telling title, *Devil Take the Hindmost*), the most eager participants in the market included "weavers, spinners, cobblers, bakers, grocers, and peasants"—that is, social classes that had never before had such easy access to a market that promised great riches. Meanwhile, tulip-bulb collectors who were truly knowledgeable about the value of their product bowed out of the market as soon as prices began climbing to ridiculous heights. The richest merchants—the vastly experienced and much-heralded Amsterdam traders who had real knowledge of supply and demand—stuck to their knitting. As Chancellor notes, they stayed away from flower bulbs and continued to invest in "town houses, East India stock, or bills of exchange—for them, tulips remained merely an expression of wealth, not a means to that end."[91]

For the spinner, cobbler, or baker who wanted to get in the game, there were certain barriers to entry, but that only made the market more enticing. In the 1620s, even before the mania gathered momentum, the most prized kind of tulip bulb, a Semper Augustus, cost about as much as a nice Amsterdam town house. It was a symbol of wealth, luxury, nobility, and best of all, a prized possession that very few people could afford. Fortunately for the masses, it became possible to "invest in" tulips using credit. Within certain rooms of some inns (called colleges), buyers and sellers would meet to agree upon prices, with the buyer paying the three-guilder commission.[92] No one got to view samples of the flowers. In fact, the buyer could not even see what he had bought until the following spring. It was sheer speculation, of the purest kind, which, in the centuries since the market went bust, has made Tulipomania one of the prime examples of a market run wild.

The profits, of course, were all on paper. (Sound familiar?) If you were a shoemaker who bought a Viceroy tulip bulb for 2,500 guilders on January 12, 1636, you wrote out a promissory note to the seller. If you'd actually had that kind of money, you could have bought, for the same price, twenty-seven tons of wheat, fifty tons of rye, four oxen, eight fat pigs, twelve fat sheep, two hogsheads of wine, four tuns of beer, two tons of butter, three tons of cheese, a bed with linen, a wardrobe of clothes, and a silver beaker.[93] The trouble was, no farmer, brewer, dairy, tailor, or silversmith would have accepted your promissory note as payment for such real goods. To find a taker for your note, you needed someone in the "college" who was just as wild about tulips as you were, and equally willing to speculate on next year's crop, sight unseen. If all went well, you were able to sell your 2,500-guilder Viceroy for 3,000 guilders or so. You'd be five hundred guilders richer *on paper*. If the person who sold you a few Viceroys actually paid up, you would be in a position to buy a beautiful town house (the McMansions of the day), settle in with your servants and finery, and live like a nobleman. It was a delightful prospect, so intoxicating that people entirely neglected to check up on whether the next debtor in line could actually afford to pay the 3,000 guilders he'd promised you. No matter. The fool who had bought the Viceroy from you was already on the lookout for a greater fool who would, in turn, purchase the nonexistent prized tulip at an even higher price.

On February 3, 1637, with spring approaching, fate revealed the greatest fools—those at the end of the line who had promised to buy Admirals and Generals and Viceroys for 4,000 or 5,000 or 6,000 guilders. When they went out looking for prospective buyers, they discovered *there were none to be found*. Why, on that day of all days, did buyers suddenly lose their confidence in the market? The answer isn't clear, though it's quite likely, as Chancellor surmises, that everyone realized that the game would be up as soon as the first spring tulips emerged from the earth. Because it was then that the greatest fool who had promised to pay the greatest price for a tulip he had never seen would be asked to fork over many thousands of guilders he didn't possess. The shoemaker didn't have anything like those riches, nor did the weaver, the cowherd, the cobbler, or the blacksmith. All the thrill he'd felt, holding the promise of those riches, vanished overnight when he went into the rooms of the inn where so many buyers had been before, and found no one else there but sellers like himself. Warren Buffett says, "Only when the tide goes out do you discover who's been swimming naked."

As in any crash, there was a rush and clamor to sell *at any price*, but no buyers. One default followed another, like a line of dominoes, and professional florists were left with nothing but rows upon rows of worthless bulbs.

Of course, this was just the moment when Hans and Jan and Vincent should have placed a call to the Dutch Treasury and asked for a Tulip Market Rescue Program sponsored by the citizens of Holland. But alas, they were not so savvy in those days, and tulip growers who were too big to fail were, in fact, allowed to collapse. Later on, as lawsuits flourished and one citizen after another declared financial ruin, a government commission was put together to arrange a settlement among the parties. But they simply decreed (in 1638) that an unfilled tulip contract could be annulled for a price equal to 3.5 percent of the promissory note. The bubble had popped.

Though many of the details are sketchy, I think it's safe to say that all the classic properties of an Arrogance Cycle were evident in this seventeenth-century example. Begin with the envy and emulation of an upper class where there was concentrated wealth—all those well-dressed merchants with their town houses and carriages who could actually afford to own and cultivate the rare and much-valued tulips. Create a market where there are rampant rumors of fantastic fortunes to be made, and then give people access to those markets (the rooms of the nearby inns) with a convivial atmosphere in which to conduct trade. Make it easy for anyone to obtain credit—as easy as filling out the equivalent of a promissory note—and make sure everyone believes that this market can only go up. Best of all, the product being traded could not be viewed, studied, or assessed. While the value of these tulips grew to many multiples, they were still nothing more than a bunch of bulbs that would flower sometime in the future. The riches were phantasmagorical, and the whole system depended on the gullibility of individuals who believed they could always find an ever-richer buyer who would take on the risk.

CYCLES UPON CYCLES

Other examples of bubbles that popped, leaving ruin in their wake, can be found throughout the annals of investment history. There was the launch of the Darien Company in the 1690s, advocated by a Scotsman who was one of the founders of the Bank of England. He sold enthusiastic Scots public shares in land located on the Isthmus of Panama.[94] A similar mania for South American property seized the British public in 1822 when an enterprising British businessman established a joint-stock mining company to extract chunks of gold "weighing from two to fifty pounds"[95] from Colombian mines. (Incredibly enough, people fell for it.)

With the advent of railway enterprises, along came new opportunities for prototypes of arrogance that lured the public into remarkably ambitious investments. (Among the most enterprising was George Hudson, chairman of Britain's York and North Midland Railway and a Member of Parliament, who celebrated victory at raising 2.5 million pounds from shareholders by chortling, "I have not told a soul what I am going to do with it!"[96]) Vast opportunities for speculation opened up in America with the expansion of railroads, speculation in gold, and the ascendancy of notorious stock market operators like Jay Gould and James Fisk.[97] All these bubbles, as well as a number of lesser ones, had their day—and their history is written in booms and busts, as rich families with deep pockets and wage earners with great ambitions were, one and all, caught up in the frenzies.

In each case, as speculation drove prices and ambitions skyward, the investors (later called suckers) became further and further removed from reality. During the inflation of the bubble, they lived not in the real world, where people labored to produce goods and services, but in a fantasy world, planted somewhere in the future, where there would be no limits on the satiation of innermost desires. In the hearts of one and all, at some point arrogance took over, and the most dangerous message of all began to travel through their brains: "I can't lose."

Dangerous, because it was wrong. So wrong. They could lose—and did.

An Exemplary Bubble

Among the most instructive of the Arrogance Cycles was the so-called South Sea Bubble, a pre–Wall Street example of a runaway market fueled by pure enthusiasm. Interestingly enough, it all started with a leap toward privatization. In January of 1720 the government of Britain made a very peculiar financial arrangement with a private entity called the South Sea Company,[98] led by a charismatic and unprincipled wheeler dealer, John Blunt.[99] Though the arrangement was not quite as complicated as credit default swaps, it was pretty ingenious for its time. Basically, the South Sea Company would take on the debt incurred by the British government and issue tradable shares in its own name. British citizens who were receiving annuities from the government would have the option of converting to the South Sea Company shares. The scheme was designed in such a way that everyone (annuitants, government, existing and prospective shareholders) would all benefit if the share price went up—which is just what happened.

Share prices that had started at £128 in early January of 1720 reached £187 by mid-February, and continued to rise as people bought shares with feverish enthusiasm.[100]

The South Sea Company was free to continue issuing stock, priced according to whatever the market would bear. It also reaped revenue from interest that the government paid to the company for taking on the debt burden. Since the South Sea Company controlled the stock, it could respond to market forces, issuing new stock whenever Blunt detected a rise in the level of public enthusiasm. Meanwhile, unbeknownst to that public, some parliamentarians, public servants, and members of the court were also granted, in the deal, the option to buy stock, a process that bears a stark resemblance to today's issuing of options to corporate insiders. (Among the beneficiaries were the chancellor, postmaster general, secretary to the treasury, and the king's German mistresses.[101]) Of course, this had a soothing effect on parliamentary discussions related to the South Sea Company, since any of the restrictions placed on the company would ultimately hurt the value of shares that were allocated to these interested parties. And the beneficiaries did not hesitate to cash in on their options.[102] In June of that year, Secretary of the Treasury Charles Stanhope secretly reaped a £249,000 profit from the company.[103]

Unfettered by any rules or regulations, the shares took off, and the company responded to demand by making more offerings—a total of four "Money Subscriptions" by year's end. If you were fortunate enough to grab one of the initial shares for £128, you were able to watch the market tick steadily upward. Within a year, the stock was into its fourth subscription, with shares being sold for £1,000.

It's not hard to imagine the enthusiastic atmosphere of the London stock market around that time, since the symptoms of that swelling bubble so closely resembled what we have experienced in more recent days. You began to notice well-publicized South Sea stock offerings appearing in local newspapers and handouts. Perhaps you were wary at first, but when you heard that members of the government and the king himself were enthusiastic supporters of the South Sea Company—and when you considered the stature of men like Secretary of the Treasury Charles Stanhope and Chancellor of the Exchequer John Aislabie, who were all for it—you began to wonder whether you might be missing out on something good. After all, these were the Greenspans of their day, and if they said there was nothing to fear, why shouldn't you join in the fun and get a share of the rewards? Your work was hard, your days long, and meanwhile, your next-door neighbor, who grabbed up a few shares in the initial offering, has just made a 300 percent profit, which enabled him to buy a new carriage, furs, jewelry for his wife, and a set of imported china.

To top it all off, the director of the South Sea Company came up with a payment plan that made investing in his stock as easy as pie. You could buy a share of stock for 20 percent down, with sixteen months to pay (in eight installments). Not only that, the South Sea Company was willing to lend money to you *on your deposits,* which meant you could get in the game for nothing down.

The upshot: When a new offering was announced and greeted with wild enthusiasm, you gathered your savings, drew upon whatever credit you had with friends, relatives, and money lenders, and appeared on opening day to get a share or two (or a dozen) in this exciting new venture. The stock certificate issued to you was extremely official-looking, with all the embossments and signatures in the right places. Reassuringly, you were not only making an apparently sound investment on your own behalf, but you were also supporting a terrific patriotic cause—contributing to the expansion of British trade and industriousness throughout the world. Talk about a win-win!

There was no holding back, and who would want to? Before long, smaller enterprises, following the lead of the South Sea Company, were springing up in the market. Bright-eyed salesmen, empowered with eloquent tongues, heralded surefire investments in such novelties as Puckle's Machine Gun, Sir Richard Steele's Fish-Pool company,[104] as well as schemes to trade in human hair, find a cure for venereal disease, and develop a "Wheel for Perpetual Motion."[105]

With so many opportunities at hand, shares in these entrepreneurial ventures were sold and traded while flocks of investors grew ever larger. Optimism flowed through every portal and drawing room. Signs of excess were everywhere. Every day more people spoke the language of arrogance, expressing a firm belief that this market could only go up.

As with the citizens of Amsterdam and Haarlem in the 1630s, so it was with the citizens of London in the 1720s. Many knew they were in jeopardy when they maxed out their lines of credit and pawned their possessions to invest in unseen properties. Many felt, instinctively, that their own actions were rash. But right up until the end, they all had confidence that there was, somewhere, a greater fool who would pay even more for these embossed sheets of paper with official-looking signatures.

Several factors contributed to the crash, when it came. In an ill-conceived attack on several other "bubble companies," the government (prodded, behind the scenes, by the South Sea directors) issued writs of prosecution that sent those stocks into a nosedive. An unexpected consequence was panic in the stock market, as over-leveraged investors began selling shares in other companies (including the South Sea Company) in order to make good on their losses.[106] Meanwhile, foreign investors became increasingly interested in new bubble companies in Germany and Holland, and they sold South Sea stock in order to participate in those new ventures. Though the company announced a richer dividend, the stock that had been worth £1,000 in June plummeted to £800 in early September. By the middle of the month it stood at £600. By the end of September 1720, the South Sea Company was selling below £200. Suddenly there were no buyers, only sellers, and those sheets of paper were headed for the dustbin.

Though the rise and fall of the South Sea Bubble spanned a single year, the disaster cast a long shadow. It would be many years before investors who had been wiped out in the crash could once again feel confident about capitalizing any venture. Most humiliating, the club of gullibility included a wide range of participants. True—some got in and out at the right time, and these few were regarded as shrewd. But confidence was severely damaged, and reputations were ruined as the breadth and depth of speculative frenzy came to light. The upward phase of arrogance was followed by a downward phase of humiliation and defeat. But, as always, whatever lessons had been learned by one generation of investors would be forgotten by the next.

BUBBLES OF OUR VERY OWN

With the establishment of stock exchanges, new opportunities arose for the boom-and-bust cycle. During the twentieth century, the more-recent history of these exchanges has also provided us with something else: data collection. Granted, the data collection of 1929 in no way resembles the towering mountains of data that accumulate in fiber-optic wires in the twenty-first century, but we do know some basic facts and figures about what has occurred in the U.S. stock market over the last century-plus. And if we're to learn anything about Arrogance Cycles, it's worth taking a look at this information.

When we think of the great stock market crash of 1929—the one that brought the American economy to its knees and ushered in the Great Depression—we're likely to think of it as a single black day when panic seized the market. It's true that the worst of it came on a single day, Tuesday, October 29, 1929. As Frederick Lewis Allen describes so vividly in *Only Yesterday,*

The big gong had hardly sounded in the great hall of the exchange at ten o'clock Tuesday morning before the storm broke in full force. Huge blocks of stock were thrown upon the market for what they would bring. Five thousand shares, ten thousand shares appeared at a time on the laboring ticker at fearful reductions in price. Not only were innumerable small traders being sold out, but big ones, too, protagonists of the new economic era who a few weeks before had counted themselves millionaires.[107]

On that day there was an unprecedented plunge. At noon, the Stock Exchange's governing committee held a secret meeting beneath the exchange floor, the governors gathering surreptitiously in order to not cause any alarm, deliberating about whether to close the exchange. They decided not to, concluding that such an action would just cause more panic. Their confidence proved unjustified. The dive that started on the 29th continued through the 30th.[108] Yes, grown men wept. Fortunes were obliterated.

Long before Black Tuesday, however, there had been many unheeded warning signs. More than a year before, on June 12, 1928, the market had taken a dip that made it appear as if reality was about to close in. The San Francisco Stock Exchange was hit first (on June 11) when some of the leading stocks plummeted—including Bank of Italy, Bank of America, and United Security.[109] On Wall Street the following day, the fifty leading stocks abruptly lost over three points after several days of steady declines. Volume was a record-breaking (for that era) five million shares, and the ticker ran almost two hours behind—which meant that traders outside of the exchange could only guess at actual prices. With only a slight nudge, it seemed, the market that had been built on waves of optimism would come crashing down. But almost miraculously, within twenty-four hours, confidence had been restored and prices started climbing again—far, far beyond the remote outskirts of real value.[110]

As early as January 25, 1928, some cautious analysts at Moody's Investors Service advised the public that stock prices were running far ahead of anticipated value; they wondered, "how much of a readjustment may be required to place the stock market in a sound position."[111] To any investor who kept his head, this would have been fair warning that stocks were wildly overpriced. And yet, throughout the spring of that year, both the public and powerful speculators continued to buy at a furious rate. In Allen's words, "the speculative fever was infecting the whole country. Stories of fortunes made overnight were on everybody's lips. . . . Wives were asking their husbands why they were so slow, why they weren't getting in on all this, only to hear that their husbands had bought a hundred shares of American Linseed that very morning."

Another tremor occurred on February 2, 1929—this one related to credit. Throughout the whole period, numerous speculators had adopted the strategies that had appeared during Tulipomania, the South Sea Bubble, and other eras of runaway speculation. They bought on credit, in many cases taking out bank loans to buy stocks on margin. The "collateral" for these loans was the stock itself, a procedure that worked fine as long as the share price increased, but became untenable if there was a fall in prices. On that day, the Federal Reserve Board made a belated attempt to put the kibosh on the practice of banks loaning out money for speculative purposes. The actual statement was unusually blunt: "The Federal Reserve Act does not, in the opinion of the Federal Reserve Board, contemplate the use of resources of the Federal Reserve Banks for the creation or extension of speculative credit."

Faced with the imminent cutoff of funding, the public had responded nervously, and there was an overnight collapse in stock prices. Now strapped by lack of funds, banks responded by raising their rates on "call money." Within a few days at the end of March, the rate for call money shot up from 12 percent to 20 percent.

Many owners of stock bought on margin had to sell quickly, and even at that, some could not make good on their loans and were forced to declare bankruptcy.[112] No doubt the collapse would have continued—and Black Tuesday would have occurred in March rather than October—but the banks interceded with an offer of relatively cheap money. To avert panic, the president of National City Bank stepped up to the plate and announced that—despite the reservations of the Federal Reserve—his bank would lend $5 million on call at the old rate of 15 percent.[113] (He offered another $15 million of call money at rates between 16 and 20 percent.) Again, confidence had been restored, panic averted, and buying on margin resumed, enabling a rise to still giddier heights.

Following any of these tremors, investors had the opportunity to get out of the market while the getting was good. (And some did. Charlie Chaplin sold all his stocks in 1928 and never reinvested.) There were voices issuing dire warnings, like investment advisor Roger Babson, who, in early September 1929, forecast a crash followed by dreadful events. "Factories will be shut down," he said. "Men will be thrown out of work . . . the vicious circle will get in full swing, and the result will be a serious business depression."[114] But despite these signals, euphoria crept back in.

The question is, why? It was all optimism, of course, and in a market like that, optimism was sure to win.

Were there reasons for such a bright outlook? Throughout the nineteenth and early twentieth centuries, there had been periods of boom and bust that took their toll on people's confidence in business and in American society. In 1913, however, the Federal Reserve System was established, and financiers predicted an era of "new economics" when crises would become, permanently, a thing of the past.[115] The newly created Federal Reserve could control interest rates, which meant that, theoretically, that it could rein in runaway inflation. It was also empowered to conduct "open market operations." As an independent agency that was not slowed down by legislative decision-making processes, the Federal Reserve could make instantaneous decisions to buy or sell government bonds to reduce or increase the money supply held by banks. Though its full powers still had to be tested in the marketplace, bankers and traders accepted the easy assumption that the Federal Reserve would henceforward protect them from cycles of boom and bust.[116]

At the beginning of the 1920s, in an era that came to be known as "Coolidge Prosperity," in honor of a president who was happy to let the market take its course, the American population as a whole was feeling enormously optimistic about the future. New goods were on the market, with cars and radios leading the list. Between 1919 and 1929, the sale of cars more than tripled, from 6,771,000 to 23,121,000.[117] Commercial radio broadcasting got started in 1920, and by 1922, $60 million worth of radios had been sold. (By 1929 that figure had increased by 1,400 percent, to $842,548,000,[118] and one out of every three homes in America had a new radio.) As the twenties roared along, so did the industries that advertised in this new medium and fed the appetite for entertainment. Stock in Radio Corporation of America became a bellwether of the new obsession with advertising, consuming, and enjoying the fruits of prosperity. In the twelve-month period between 1928 and 1929, its stock rose by more than 600 percent, from a low of 85.25 to a high of 549.[119] This was the life—fed steadily by rising demand and an ever-increasing supply of credit to the average consumer.[120] Though the credit card was still a thing of the future, stores willingly allowed people to spread out their payments over time, and bankers were eager to make loans for cars and homes.

As for brokers, businessmen, and advertisers, all thrived on media saturation. The novelty of the radio meant that many people were listening, and the popularity of local and regional papers meant that advertisers could reach everyone. Rumors spread fast, tastes changed quickly, and the models of wealth and fashion were instantly in the public eye.

As for the sale of stocks, no advertising was needed. Rumors spread. Credit was available. Word was, this was a market that could only go up—and people believed it. At the same time, many barriers to investment were lowered. Brokerage houses opened up all across the United States.[121] Loans were readily available to purchase stocks. In 1927 alone, more than $740 million was loaned to brokers to carry margin accounts for traders—a huge amount in those days. (The total outstanding in margin accounts, by the end of that year, exceeded $3.5 billion.)[122] Though the Federal Reserve cautioned its member banks against making loans to brokers for speculation, there was no enforcement, and as long as the market kept rising, speculators were willing to pay more for their margin loans.[123] Access became even easier as investment trusts were established, luring in new investors with promises of sound management while the managers pursued high-risk strategies that created enormous excess turnover.[124]

Of course, as in any market of this kind, there were many cheerleaders. Men like Charles Mitchell, one of the leading speculators, who called the stock market "a weather-vane pointing into a gale of prosperity," and, on the eve of the Crash, declared that there was "nothing fundamentally wrong with the stock market or the underlying business or credit structure."[125] There were also tales of kingpins who had struck it rich, such as William Crapo Durant, the founder of General Motors, who created an investment pool said to be worth more than $4 billion and reaped an estimated $100 million in profits.[126] Ninety percent of the nation's wealth was in the hands of 5 percent of the population, but by means of speculation, everyone saw an opportunity to become part of that club. The voices of skeptics were drowned out by general enthusiasm. This was a market that promised to keep going up, and those foretelling an end to it all were nothing but Cassandras. Criticism was more than a sin; it was also in bad taste. For America to succeed, believers were needed.

◆

Let me pause, here, to say that the position of a skeptic, under circumstances like these, is no fun at all. I experienced the discomfort firsthand in 1999, when I was the go-to curmudgeon for many of my friends in business news. It was the peak of the dot-com frenzy. Amazon.com would rally thirty points in a day, and some old-school company would add "dot-com" to its name and prices would rally 20 percent. Reporters called nonstop because I didn't believe the hype. I refused to accept a "new paradigm" where earnings and balance sheets didn't matter. When I suggested that these new Internet companies would be like the automobile companies of the 1900s, I meant it was likely that 85 percent of them would fail over time.

During the late 1990s when these tech stocks were screaming, we took a small position for clients in a little-known company that offered something called CDMA. CDMA allowed computers to communicate with several devices at once. Prior to CDMA, if your computer was printing, you couldn't use it for anything else until your printing job was complete. The company was Qualcomm, and the gains were staggering.

The tech bubble began to burst in 1999, and the slide continued into 2000. Qualcomm was outrageously expensive, and our discipline had us selling shares at regular intervals. We waited on our largest sale until January 3, 2000, in order to delay the tax burden for another year. Qualcomm was near its all-time high. We felt great.

Shortly after the Qualcomm triumph, we received notice that we were being fired by a small-business-owner client in Baltimore. While we had selected and bought the stock in his account and had done all of the ongoing, additional research, he felt like he knew much more than we did about how to manage his money. He was furious that we'd sold his Qualcomm. He complained that he'd made a fortune on it and wanted to let it increase. Moreover, he said that the NASDAQ had gained something like 70 percent in the previous year, and though we had exceeded the S&P 500, he was firing us and moving his money 100 percent into NAS-DAQ and tech stocks. (As it turned out, his timing was tragically off; that firing marked the 5100 peak of the NASDAQ and the tipping point of the tech-stock bubble.)

That business owner was not the only one to lambaste me. During that period, plenty of investors seemed to think I was off my rocker. "Farr doesn't get it at all. There has been a generational paradigm shift to new-concept companies," one critic said. What the hell was he talking about? I wasn't sure. Neither was Warren Buffett (so I was in pretty good company). They attacked Buffett by saying that he was an old man, starting to miss a few beats, who just couldn't keep up in this new, marvelous, but complex world. Poor old Warren! My cautious advice was mocked. People invested in the notion of a new paradigm wouldn't or couldn't bear skepticism or questioning. They had to be right. Their blinders were firmly in place and they were running at breakneck speed. And, dear reader, necks were broken.

There were certainly plenty of those. No expectations were too high, no amount of wealth was considered excessive. It looked as if everyone could share in the bounty. A lot like the atmosphere—I imagine—that existed seventy years earlier in 1929.

◆

The pop of the bubble in 1929 brought about the usual emotions: first, disbelief, and then, sheer panic. Had stock speculation been confined to Wall Street brokers and traders, the damage might have been curtailed. But by 1929 speculation was ubiquitous. Though the word *investment* had become meaningless—prices were so out of line with any reasonable price/earnings ratios—millions of people now considered themselves to be investors. With the collapse of the market came the dreaded sinking of expectations. Margin calls could not be met. As with the end of all bubbles, there was a domino effect as paper fortunes disappeared overnight. Afterward, there were many Monday-morning quarterbacks, not the least of which was John Maynard Keynes. "The position is serious," he wrote in 1936, "when enterprise becomes a bubble on a whirlpool of speculation. When the capital development of a country becomes a by-product of the activities of a casino, the job is likely to be ill done."[127]

How did it happen? How did so many people become so deluded? What were the causes of the Crash?

It was an era with all the hallmarks of arrogance—the optimism, the excesses, and the firm belief that the market could detach itself from reality and prices could continue going up indefinitely. And there was that other ingredient that appeared on the scene in the Roaring Twenties—a sense of entitlement. Everyone thought they deserved the rewards. Those rewards were to be found in a market that "could only go up." As in every Arrogance Cycle, people actually came to believe that they were superhuman and that the limitations of gravity did not apply to them.

CHAPTER 6

INSIDER ARROGANCE

The World May Be Flat, But It's Not Even!

You're invited to a dice game—but before you say whether you'll play or not, let me present a couple of options.

We can either go to Vince's Place or to Bernie's Place. Vince's Place, I've got to admit, is nothing special. It's clean and well-lit; the food is decent, but it's not the most comfortable joint. It gets raucous sometimes, and the players can be rude. The usual stuff. The only thing is, I can guarantee you the game will be fair. I don't mean you'll win all the time. That's impossible—we're talking *dice*, a game of chance. No one wins all the time. That's the point. But I can guarantee that these aren't loaded dice. The house is not skimming off the top. No special favors for guys who have been there the longest. This is a fair-and-square game, and your risks are just the same as the next guy's. Your chances of winning, or losing, are no better or worse than those of anyone else in the room.

Bernie's Place is a whole different scene. Much classier, great food, comfortable seating—the whole bit. I guarantee you, you'll have a great time at Bernie's. In fact, if you talk to the right people at Bernie's Place, you'll have more than a great time. You'll also have a chance of making something on the side. Yes, it's true; the dice at Bernie's aren't quite what they should be. It still looks like a game of chance, but if you know whom to talk to, and when, you can tilt the odds just a little bit in your favor. Not so it's very noticeable; not so you'll get caught and be thrown out of the room. Just a slight edge that makes you a winner more often than not. Sure, that means some others are going to lose out more often than they should, but hey, this is dice, not chapel. You'll come out ahead. That's the main thing. One of my golf buddies always jokes that all he asks for is a fair advantage. He'd like Bernie's Place.

So there you go. Choose. Where do you want to play? Vince's Place? Or Bernie's?

◆

As I've mentioned, I was once invited to St. Petersburg to act as an advisor and consultant in helping to start up the St. Petersburg stock exchange. This was the Gorbachev era, when the Soviet Union was disintegrating and millions of Russians had begun to embark on the stormy seas of capitalist enterprise. The stock exchange was in its infancy. Most, if not all, of its traders were accustomed to doing things the old way. Bribery and corruption were rampant. They would look at you like you were out of your mind if you invested in a company where you didn't have insider information or couldn't bribe someone for special considerations. Insider trading—sharing privileged knowledge to get a leg up on a deal—was as common and customary as a shot of vodka. If you knew someone who could tell you something, you used your influence or your rubles to apply some pressure, extract the information you needed, and then proceed to place your bet on the stock that you already knew was going to be rising.

When I talked to these guys about the concept of a stock market where certain rules applied, they genuinely thought they were dealing with a raving lunatic. Why would you throw away a perfectly good opportunity to make money when you could take advantage of your privileged position and profit thereby? Why take the same kinds of risk that other people were taking when you could talk to some old apparatchiks, do some favors at the right moments, and come out ahead? It was stupid, they said, to undergo needless doubt and uncertainty when, with the greasing of a few palms, you could lock in your profits and go home happy.

I understood their attitude. I even had a label for it: Insider Arrogance. In their world, it was an invariable part of doing business based on inarguable assumptions: Privilege has its rewards. It's better to act smart than look stupid. Risk is an unnecessary part of the game. The whole idea was to load the dice in your own favor so you'd shave your risk and beat the odds.

They were in Bernie's Place, and couldn't imagine being anyplace else.

Two things I tried to explain: first, the advantage of having certain rules ("playing fair" would be the old-fashioned term for it), and second, the advantage of adhering to those rules. Not easy concepts to get across, especially in that environment. In fact, I know they regarded me as lame for even bringing it up. The whole point of the capitalist system, in their view, was to make money, and that's just what they were doing—wasn't it? What was this talk about "a level playing field"—this nonsense about "transparency"? They felt they understood that competition was fundamental to the American way of doing things. The whole idea was to get an edge over the other guy and then to take all you could get for yourself. They had just been liberated from a system that wore itself out paying lip service to "the common good," and now they had to listen to an American who was advocating the kind of stock exchange setup that would follow rules and regulations and give everyone a fair chance. What was I—some kind of commie?

I had to admit, they had a point. Those guys in St. Petersburg were making money in ways that were customary and familiar to them. Spotting opportunities and grabbing; buying confidential information and using it for personal advantage; seeing weaknesses in the system and using the leverage of their position for profit. All very competitive. Dogfighting with the leashes off.

But there was something they *didn't* get, and it was a bit difficult to explain to them—at least too bluntly—without being insulting.

The problem was this: Who the hell would want to risk their money in the kind of stock exchange these guys were running? Sure, the U.S. system had its flaws, but if you had a choice between putting your money in the St. Petersburg Stock Exchange versus putting it in the New York Stock Exchange, count on it: You'd be taking on infinitely more risk if you went to Russia.

Fact is, you'd have to be nuts. Place your bets in a joint where half the guys were in cahoots against you? Where insider trading and double-dealing and skimming were the order of the day? Would you want to try to figure out the best-run companies with the optimum price/earnings ratios when you couldn't even get basic information about who was running them, how they were managed, or what their sales were? Good luck. As gently as possible, I had to break the news to these guys: "You know, you may be having a great time, and those new Rolexes you're wearing might even be the real thing, but as long as you're playing by your own rules—which means, no rules—I think you're going to have quite a bit of trouble attracting foreign investment. There just aren't a lot of people who want to spend time in Bernie's Place. And that's not likely to change until you take some measures to convince investors around the globe that they can actually trust you guys."

Insider trading is a term of art and not a legal term. The definition, therefore, is imprecise but generally accepted. It means trading with the advantage of material nonpublic information. *Material* is understood as significant to a reasonable investor when deciding to buy or sell. During the 2008 financial crisis, Goldman Sachs was accused (and later settled with the Securities and Exchange Commission) of selling a synthetic collateralized debt obligation that had been perfected to fail by a portfolio manager who wanted to make a bet on the downside. Goldman was accused of encouraging some of their customers to buy so that their other client could sell, but did not disclose that this type of bond had been essentially created to fail. The SEC alleged that this information would have been material to those getting stuck with this garbage. The filing resulted in a $500 million settlement (the largest in history) by Goldman Sachs, who neither admitted nor denied guilt. Goldman Sachs felt that the buyers were very sophisticated institutions that reviewed each of the components of the security prior to purchase. They posited that the purpose for the security's structure was unimportant.

I don't know about you, but I'd like to know if I were being encouraged to buy something that had been expertly designed to fail. But that's just me.

THE PREMIUM ON FAIR PLAY

The world may be flat, but it's not even. We still have choices. Vince's Place or Bernie's Place? I favor Vince's Place, and I'm not alone. So, historically, do most investors who have an interest in knowing what they're dealing with when they are playing with a portion of their life savings. Don't get me wrong: There are no sure things in Vince's Place. You're still betting, and there's still risk. But for the most part, what investors are looking for is a fair game where the same rules apply to all. And that just ain't the way it's done at Bernie's Place.

During the better part of the twentieth century, we knew where to go for a game that was—if not perfect—at least the fairest game in town. Following the 1929 stock market crash, which had worldwide repercussions, both the U.S. government and the New York Stock Exchange implemented some rules, regulations, and customary practices that served pretty well for quite a few decades. Their design, in effect, helped to guard against the kind of Insider Arrogance that you'd find at Bernie's Place. Commercial banks were prohibited from participating heavily in high-risk stock, bond, and currency gambles. Traders were prohibited from buying large blocks of stocks on margin. Companies got into the habit of issuing audited reports that revealed capitalization, income, earnings, expenses, depreciation, write-downs, and other relevant accounting arcana. Professionally run commissions were set up to ride herd on such aberrations as Ponzi schemes, shell companies, and insider trading. The Federal Reserve System was created to help maintain financial stability in monetary matters, intervening as necessary, at the discretion of the chairman and officers, to help rein in inflation (when necessary), tighten lending (when advisable), smooth out recessions, and theoretically, guard against bubbles. As a result, in the years since 1929, while there have been stock market crashes (1973–74, 1987, 2000, and 2008), we never again experienced the kind of horrible plunge that occurred on Black Tuesday and the days following.

And the reward for maintaining this generally clean, well-lit place? Considerable. From all around the world, trillions upon trillions in foreign currency have been exchanged for dollars, many of which are invested in U.S. exchanges. The New York Stock Exchange is a bustling place. Where a record-breaking day in the 1920s was 5 million shares traded, an average day in 2010 was close to 1.6 billion.[128] Despite all the hiccups in the economy brought on by wars, hurricanes, recessions, scandals, and al Qaeda attacks, the market has shown steady growth since the low of 1929. Investors who tried their hand in the shakier exchanges have returned, time and again, to the United States as a bastion of security. Over the long haul, Vince's Place has attracted a far better quality of clientele and reaped far higher profits than Bernie's.

So, in the long term, it has paid off. Those rules we put in place after 1929 have helped. The tradition of rendering audited quarterly reports on the companies that are listed on the exchange, the flow of information from executive offices to consumers, the regulations against insider trading and the punishments meted out for fraud and conspiracy—all of these measures, plus a few more, have created an environment in which people around the world have wanted to do business.

The question is, will it continue to be that way?

In the past couple of decades, we have been chagrined to witness what happens when some of the fundamental rules are altered and when some game-changing strategies are allowed to go unchecked. Basically, there have been three big changes in the past decade: The first was an act of Congress that resulted in the revoking of the Glass-Steagall Act in 1999; second, the gradual, subtle coercion of accounting firms accompanied by the increased inability of auditors to keep pace with the creative work of financial officers, lawyers, and other parties with a vested interest in concealment; and third, the sharp rise of Insider Arrogance, which has essentially made it impossible for the Securities and Exchange Commission to do its job.

It is instructive, I think, to see the impact of each of these changes on Vince's Place.

THE SLIPPING OF GLASS-STEAGALL

On November 12, 1999, Charles Glass would have turned over in his grave. That was the date when President Bill Clinton, flanked by grinning representatives Phil Gramm, Jim Leach, and Thomas J. Bliley Jr., formally signed the Gramm-Leach-Bliley Act (the "Financial Services Modernization Act of 1999") that spelled the repeal of the Glass-Steagall Act of 1933.[129]

Did I say Charlie Glass would have simply turned over? No, that gesture would be much too modest for a man renowned for his fiery eloquence, deep convictions, and strong sense of mission. Glass would have done far more. He would have risen from his grave, shaken off the dust of decades, donned his double-breasted gray suit, adjusted his broad colorful tie over his modestly pro-truding potbelly, and risen up in front of those self-satisfied, self-deluded jerks. His Napoleon-size frame would have undoubtedly quivered with righteous indignation. *You idiots!* he would have bellowed, his syllables tinged with the slight drawl of a Virginia gentleman waxing furious. *You've set back the clock sixty years! You're making the same damn mistakes those greedy speculators made in my day when they destroyed the banks, wiped out the economy, brought death and destruction and hunger and despair down on the heads of millions of Americans. Cease this NOW!* I imagine him wresting the pen from Clinton's hand. *Stop messing around with what you don't understand! If you sign this bill, you're going to unleash all the pow-ers of destruction that brought us to our knees in 1929. All my good work—down the drain! Fools! Imbeciles! Morons!*

If only.

If only Glass could have risen from his grave, said those things, stopped them in their tracks, shaken them from their lobbyist-induced torpor and their theory-induced convictions. But alas, he was not there. It did not happen. Instead, the bill was signed. Grins and handshakes were shared all around. And the course was set for a financial collapse that was, indeed, as grave as the one that occurred in 1929 (and could have been far worse).

Who was this guy, Glass? Why did he fight so hard for the bill that bore his name, and why would he have been so disgusted and ashamed to see his hard work go up in smoke?

Charlie Glass, born in 1858 in Lynchburg, Virginia,[130] the son of the owner of the *Lynchburg Daily Republican,* seemed destined from birth to follow the same calling as his father. At the age of twenty-two, he became a reporter for the *Lynchburg News,* and was promoted to editor in 1887. He later bought out that paper as well as two competing papers in town, to become the sole daily-newspaper publisher in Lynchburg. Then his career took a turn. Glass became increasingly involved in politics, and in 1902 he was elected to the U.S. House of Representatives. By 1913 Glass was chairman of the House Committee on Banking and Currency. He got along well with President Woodrow Wilson, a fellow Democrat and Virginian, who appointed him secretary of the treasury five years later. In 1920 he was appointed to fill a seat in the U.S. Senate, a position he was to hold until his death in 1946. His career in politics, therefore, stretched across eight presidential administrations, spanning the crash of 1907, World War I, the creation of the Federal Reserve System, the Roaring Twenties, the Crash of 1929, the Great Depression, and World War II.

Throughout his tenure, the economy was his obsession. Having lived through the devastating crash of 1907 and having witnessed, as a journalist and congressman, the inner workings of the economy, Glass unhesitatingly labeled the United States as having "the most barbarous financial system on earth." Glass set out to fix it. Working with members of the Wilson administration and the president himself, Glass was instrumental in bringing the Federal Reserve System into being. He argued strongly for an independent body that could exercise some control over monetary policy, encourage or curb bank borrowing, help keep a lid on inflation, and, in general, play a policing role over the economy.[131] With the signing of the Federal Reserve Act on December 23, 1913,[132] Charlie Glass won his first great legislative victory. Ever the journalist, he went on to write a book published in 1923, entitled *The Federal Reserve: A Study of the Banking System of the United States.* (The 1,000-page tome was *not* a best seller.)

Toward the end of the 1920s, then-senator Glass began to notice dangerous signs of a runaway stock market. It was February 1929 when he declared, "The great corporations of the country have acquired the habit of throwing their surplus funds into the vortex of stock speculation, instead of distributing them among their stockholders in the nature of dividends, and individuals are doing the same thing." His reservations were deep-seated. "Member banks of the system have manipulated their deposit accounts so as to transfer from the demand deposit account, requiring a reserve of 7 percent, to the time deposit account, requiring a reserve of only 3 percent, thereby releasing enormous funds to be thrown into the maelstrom of stock speculation." Though his voice was strong, the Arrogance Cycle of the twenties was reaching its full height, and—like many other warnings—his was drowned out in the general clamor.

What particularly worried Glass, as his words reveal, was the involvement of the entire banking industry in the excesses of Wall Street. The follies and foibles of stockbrokers were their own business, as he saw it, but he balked at the sight of banks using the money of their trusting depositors in order to make wild bets on a runaway market. "Unless some man be wise enough, and have wit enough to give a statutory definition of investments as contradistinguished from stock gambling," he raged, "I do not see how we are to curb these gambling activities."[133]

Prior to the Crash, his warnings were regarded as not much more than a rant. As long as the market was steadily going up, banks were making plenty of money by leveraging mortgage payments and savings deposits of moms, pops, and kids from heartland America, using that solid base of funding to take part in the high-stakes game of American roulette that was being played on Wall Street. Then came the Crash, and all of a sudden Charlie Glass didn't seem like such a nutcase. What he had foretold came true. Banks that had loaned money on margin or used assets for stock market speculation were wiped out. As depositors lined up to withdraw their life savings and the banks slammed their doors shut, sending moms and pops back home empty-handed, Glass once again climbed very high on his soapbox and began advocating a bill that suddenly seemed to make a lot of sense. Separate the *commercial* banks from the *investor* banks, he said. Separate the banking entities that finance speculators and gamblers and investors from the banks that finance mortgages and businesses and secured loans.

How to make this happen? It was not a matter of asking the bankers very politely whether they would please keep their gambling separate from their savings, or take better care of the moms and pops who were trusting them. Nope. Glass, former journalist and the fire-spouting politician from Virginia, wouldn't trust banks and speculators any more than he'd trust the petty thief in cell number four of the county jail. If you wanted to get bankers and speculators to separate savings from speculation, there was only one way to do it: You had to have laws, and the laws had to be enforced. Who could create a law that would apply to every bank in the entire nation? It had to be Congress. When was the best time to pass a law like that? Right on the heels of the greatest market crash in history, when everyone could clearly see the awful consequences of banking practices run amok. The best guy to propose that law? Charlie Glass.

Even in the midst of the grim Depression, however, Glass had a hard time pushing his bill through. Fortunately, this little guy with his big tie, bulbous nose, and loud voice was indefatigable. He introduced the bill into the Senate on January 22, 1932, where it was met with a storm of resistance from a wide consortium of protestors who had an interest in the stock market—not only brokers and investors, but also bankers and politicians. The bill was withdrawn in time for the national conventions of both national parties, then reintroduced by Glass with the support of Henry B. Steagall of Alabama, who was chairman of the House Committee on Banking and Currency. Steagall wanted one important addition: an agreement to permit bank deposit insurance. With that in place, the act took on the name Glass-Steagall and was passed the following year.[134]

Though the bill was somewhat watered down during passage, it was pretty much the way Charlie had wanted it. Two of its most important provisions went like this:

1. To provide the Federal Reserve Board with greater control over speculative credit by giving it power to impose penalties, one penalty being to suspend credit facilities of the System to any member bank which ignored official warnings against increasing outstanding collateral loans while obtaining 15-day advances from a Federal Reserve Bank on its promissory note.

2. Security affiliates of banks were to be brought under strict supervision by the Federal Reserve Board; and it was required that they be completely divorced within three years.[135]

Other provisions dealt with such details as the makeup of the Federal Open Market Committee, measures to increase branch banking, and the creation of a "Federal liquidating corporation" that could oversee the orderly closing of member banks that were in distress. The bill also specified that banks in smaller communities (e.g., the ones handling home mortgages and small-business loans) were required to increase their minimum reserves.

A lot of speculators were unhappy, and so were many bankers, but as time went on, and the law *was* enforced, they got used to it. Moms and pops began to feel confident once again that they could put their money in local banks that wouldn't use it to buy wildly inflated shares of Radio Corporation of America, General Motors, American Can, or Montgomery Ward. Speculators got liquidity from investment banks that began to take on a character and reputations of their own—where one savvy insider could settle a deal with a phone call to someone equally in the know, and together they would ride the roller coaster of the market to serve their own ends. For speculators, the roller-coaster ride was still bumpy. For moms, pops, and enterprising small-business owners, well, they still had to pay off loans and build up savings, but at least their ho-hum accounts were safe from vandals, gamblers, and swindlers. It wasn't a perfect banking world under Glass-Steagall, but it was good enough. And Glass could go to his grave (which he did, in 1946) well satisfied that he'd put a stop to one hell of a lousy practice, making life feel a lot more secure for his fellow Virginians and millions of other Americans. Glass-Steagall turned U.S. markets into Vince's Nation.

BROKEN GLASS

The Glass-Steagall Act remained in force, as a customary and usual part of the banking landscape, until 1986. In that year, however, some unhappy bankers began to fiddle around with it.

The trouble started when Bankers Trust started to get bored with solid old banking practices and decided it was high time the company made some real money. Being as susceptible to envy and ambition as anyone else, BT was piqued that firms like Goldman Sachs and Lehman Brothers could play for big stakes in a game that was off-limits for banks (because of the pesky Glass-Steagall Act). The directors at Bankers Trust began to yearn for more glittery-looking end-of-the-year results, but they couldn't dally with investments unless they got permission to raise the limits on the proportion of assets they could use for speculation. This they endeavored to do. Hard lobbying, combined with lots of phone calls in the right places, got them at least partway to where they wanted to go. And under Federal Reserve Board Chairman Paul Volcker, Glass-Steagall was amended to allow Bankers Trust to engage in some unsecured, short-term credit transactions, so long as this business did not become "a large proportion of revenue."[136]

What harm, it was thought, could this possibly do? For an institution like Bankers Trust, putting a mere 5 percent of assets at risk seemed negligible. Even in a worst-case scenario, if the bank lost 100 percent of its investment in unsecured loans, it would not be mortally wounded.

True enough, but there was a greater significance: The dike had been breached. The great persuaders, all the bankers who had not been able to play with the big boys, got the first whiffs of a mighty temptation. If a bank could use 5 percent of its assets to get in the game—well, why not 20 percent, or 30 percent?

Sure enough, on February 7, 1987, there was a big sit-down with eight bankers, a number of Wall Street financiers, and Paul Volcker's Federal Reserve Board. Volcker himself was opposed to any further loosening of restrictions, but he was faced with a formidable array of bank executives representing (among others) J.P. Morgan, Citicorp, and (back again for more) Bankers Trust. All wanted the Fed to allow them to move into forbidden territory, including commercial paper (short-term unsecured loans to businesses); municipal revenue bonds; and what would prove to be most dangerous of all, mortgage-backed securities. When pressed to explain how conditions had changed since 1933 when Glass-Steagall had been enacted, the vice chairman of Citicorp, Thomas C. Theobald, argued that there were three factors: a Securities and Exchange Commission that he described as "very effective" when it came to enforcement; investors who were more knowledgeable than their 1920s brethren; and ratings agencies that were so "sophisticated" that nothing escaped their scrutiny.

It was Insider Arrogance at its peak, and a majority of the members of the Federal Reserve Board bought into it. Volcker staunchly opposed the proposal, saying he feared that lenders would "recklessly lower loan standards in pursuit of lucrative securities offerings and market bad loans to the public." But he was outvoted, 3–2, and in early 1987 the Federal Reserve Board moved to ease the regulations that had been imposed under the Glass-Steagall Act.[137]

The barn door flew open. The fields were ripe for picking. By March of 1987, the Fed voted to allow Chase Manhattan Corporation to join Bankers Trust in lending commercial paper through a financial subsidiary. In August of that year, President Reagan appointed Alan Greenspan to be chairman of the Federal Reserve Board. A former director of J.P. Morgan, Greenspan was all for banking deregulation. With Volcker replaced, the final resistance evaporated. By early 1989, the Federal Reserve was allowing banks to create "security affiliates" that could "raise money for corporations in the bond market."[138] It was precisely what Charles Glass had fought, tooth and nail, some fifty years earlier. Though there was still a 10 percent limit on the assets that could be used in this way, it was only a matter of time before those limits were eased once again. In December 1996, Greenspan and the board raised the limit to 25 percent—which, for most of the big banks, opened the way to virtually unlimited spending in the securities business.[139] In the fall of 1998 a merger between Citicorp and Travelers was approved by the Federal Reserve Board. I was called to CNN for my reaction, which was: *If bigger is better, these guys will be the BEST.* I was stunned by the size and scope of this new behemoth. Most vexing to me was the prospect of monitoring and coordinating so many divisions and employees and types of risk in several different countries and currencies. It was no longer possible to see any daylight between commercial banking, investment banking, and the insurance business. All that remained was to repeal Glass-Steagall and have done with it.

The coup de grace, when it came, was by a margin of one vote. In May of 1998, the House voted 214–213 on a bill that eliminated the walls between banks, securities firms, and insurance companies. In the Senate, the Banking Committee introduced some compromises, but a final version of the bill revoking Glass-Steagall was passed on November 4, 1999, and signed into law eight days later.[140]

True, some legislators still had concerns that the commercial side of the bank could give valuable information to the trading side, so regulators established a handy rule: There must be, they said, a firewall (known on Wall Street as "the Chinese Wall") between one side of the bank and the other. And, they pleaded, waving their fingers, there must be no passing of secret notes back and forth over the wall.

How was this rule to be enforced? Simple; just ask. "No notes! No gossip!" If you ask them not to do it, they won't do it. Right?

Unfortunately, Glass was long gone, or he would have stopped the nonsense right there. But the memory of his dire warnings was eclipsed by the more up-to-date philosophy of men like Greenspan, great believers in an open market that would be policed by intelligent self-interest. Their views held sway.

So a cheerful Bill Clinton signed the Gramm-Leach-Bliley Act (aka, the Financial Services Modernization Act) into law with the stroke of a pen, and Charlie Glass turned over in his grave. All across America, bankers rejoiced. They could play again at last. Arrogance had won the day.

Of course, in the first flush of victory, no one could have anticipated the catastrophe that was to come.

THE ACCOUNTANTS WHO GOT CREATIVE

Meanwhile, back at the office, a great number of financial officers and accountants were also doing their part to pave the way to catastrophe.

With the rise of Insider Arrogance, the old-fashioned tradition of customary accounting practices began to take on interesting characteristics. One problem brought to light by Andersen's flubbing of the Global Crossing, Qwest Communications, WorldCom, and Enron accounts was the close dependence of accounting firms (particularly the big ones) on the customers they serve. Working with clients who brought in many millions of dollars of earnings, accounting firms have proved themselves unable to maintain any semblance of arm's-length relationships. The accountant-client relationship becomes even trickier when—as with Andersen—the same firm offers consulting services along with auditing services. As Barbara Ley Toffler, former head of the Ethics and Responsible Business Practices Group at Andersen, observed in her account of the crack-up of the company,[141] "Traditionally, consultants had been rainmakers and auditors were supposed to be watchdogs. Now the auditors, guardians of the public trust, were becoming consulting shills. Their culture of upstanding respectability was disintegrating, but many audit partners tried to hold on to the symbols of the past while trying to keep pace with the new world outside their doors."

Objectivity went out the window—along with a lot of investigative skills—when the folks at Andersen were pressured by men like Jeff Skilling to give their seal of approval to the creation of a new entity or to report the profitability of the company as a whole. Eventually, revelations about Andersen's relationship with these clients would spell ruin for the firm. But while the Andersen story may be unique in some respects, it points to an ongoing dilemma that now confronts every accounting firm: When the pressure to maintain good relationships with a powerful client is greater than or equal to the obligation to give fair, accurate, and certifiable reports to investors, stockholders, and the general public, accountants are in the crosshairs—which is when they often do what anyone in the crosshairs would do: They duck.

Another problem with the accountant's position, however, has less to do with conscience and more to do with the very nature of the job itself. No matter how large or small the company reported on, or the company doing the reporting, there is one phrase that is too often excluded from the lexicon of an accountant's vocabulary. That phrase is, "I don't know." And yet, "I don't know" is, in many cases, the only accurate, appropriate, and meaningful response to the dazzling complexity of many corporate practices and subsidiary relationships. In submitting a truly comprehensive and honest audit of a company as large and complex as Enron, there should have been many admissions of ignorance on the part of the Andersen accountants. Deals they could not comprehend. Transactions they were not allowed to view. Assumptions (right or wrong) that were made in the auditing process and questions that were left unanswered. Needless to say, had they made such admissions, they would have been fired by Enron. But if Andersen managers had been able to declare, "Don't know! Couldn't find out!" at least the reports would have been honest.

Needless to say, it's inconceivable that any accounting firm will admit that policies, actions, or details are unverifiable or incomprehensible. And yet it is precisely this level of honesty that is necessary if any outsider is to get a true picture of the degree of risk involved when investing in many companies. What is the risk in a multinational corporation's exposure to currency fluctuations? Can any accountant in the complex world of currency trading decide whether there are effective and adequate hedges for that risk? If a bank is dealing in derivatives, what are they worth on any given day? What are the potential liabilities of a company that is involved in deep-well oil drilling? To these questions, and many others, the only reasonable, rational, and accurate response is, "I don't know."

But show me an accountant who says that more than once, and I'll show you an accountant who is permanently unemployed.

Accounting practices have not kept up because they can't. In many industries, the speed and complexity of business has far out-stripped any reasonable ability to provide an accurate report of all facets of an operation. To pretend that every transaction is known, that every stone has been turned over, is just arrogant. And yet, for all practical purposes, this is exactly what accountants are still required to do, year after year, for one industry after another, as they deal with companies that are undergoing changes too rapid to calculate. No wonder we have to be skeptical. The next Enron,

I'm sure, is right under our nose, but it won't be an accountant who sniffs it out.

In the months before Enron exploded, I was on a flight to the West Coast. My analysts dreaded these trips because I would take a briefcase full of research and annual reports and return with lots of new ideas and work assignments for them. I read about Enron, and it looked fabulous. I read a quarterly report and several Wall Street research pieces. The shares were very inexpensive, and earnings were increasing at a remarkably strong rate. The history looked great, too.

As stocks were tumbling from the post-dot-com boom, I was desperate for new growth ideas. I handed my piles of highlighted research to my analysts and asked for a quick turnaround. After a week (which was not quick), they reported that they had no idea how Enron was making its money. I somewhat angrily told them that the rest of Wall Street had figured it out and to get their MBA- and CFA-credentialed asses back to their offices and figure it out. A week later, they slunk into my office and said, "Boss, there is no way to determine how this company is making its money. If it's still one of our rules that we have to understand how a company is making money, we can't begin to understand Enron." Of course, they also reminded me (though I didn't need reminding) that the decision was mine. "You can always fire us and/or buy it anyway."

I didn't violate our discipline as much as I wanted to, and the two analysts got bonuses. After Enron failed and thousands of employees lost their pensions, and investors around the world were decimated by the failure of the seventh-largest U.S. corporation, I was enraged to think that if two thirty-year-old MBAs in Washington, D.C., could figure out Enron in two weeks, what in God's name were the rest of our Wall Street brethren doing?

THE WEARY WATCHDOGS OF WALL STREET

Suppose we put you in charge of policing the dice games. It's up to you to find out who's cheating and who's playing fair and square. Who follows the rules? Who doesn't? Find out who's using loaded dice and turn them in for questioning. You'll be a hero if you do it right, the Wyatt Earp of Wall Street, making the frontier safe for honest folks (and all that).

Oh, but wait a minute. In this job description, we should mention a few limitations. You can't inspect the dice unless you suspect something is fishy, and before you do an inspection, all the players are alerted so they know you're coming in. I should also mention that you're grossly outnumbered in terms of the number of games you have to inspect relative to the number of inspectors under your command. The number of players is in the hundreds of thousands. Basically, you're outmatched. The best you can do is to try and keep up with the rumors. By the time you've gotten to the source of the rumor and ascertained whether there's any substance to it, you'll find that a few dozen *more* crap games have sprung up all over town. Just try to keep up!

(A branch manager friend at a major Wall Street wirehouse lamented that his job as a compliance supervisor was like being a lifeguard at the kiddy pool and having to know which kid was peeing in the pool. He well knew that damn near all of them were peeing.)

And another thing: I should also mention that, even though it's your job to crack down on crime, every once in a while your bosses will remind you not to be too tough because, if you are, you'll drive the players out of town, which is bad for business.

A few other things to note before you take on this job. You'll see a lot of stuff going on that looks like theft and graft and larceny, but unless you can really document and prove it, I wouldn't advise you to go in there issuing warrants because they'll shoot you down so fast you won't know what hit you. That said, if you don't do your job, and someone else catches the thieves in mid-larceny, you'll be called before a group of inquisitors and asked to explain why you weren't the first to spot the bad guys and arrest them. But I should also mention that if you do get the evidence to round them up and throw them in the clink, you'll be pretty well detested by all the guys running dice games all over town. And just to add insult to injury, those are guys who make about a thousand times what you make.

Sound like a job you want?

Welcome to the SEC.

From the time the Securities and Exchange Commission was established in 1934,[142] it's always had too much to do, while never quite having sufficient means to do it. Initially, the fundamental duty of this governmental watchdog organization was to oversee the financial markets and to help protect investors from scams. As the years passed, additional duties were added to the SEC roster. It was also expected to monitor interstate holding companies that had subsidiaries in the oil, gas, or electricity industries (1935). It was required to make sure that all investment advisors adhere to SEC regulations (1940). It was supposed to identify and prosecute cases of insider trading and investigate stock exchange operations. And, with the passage of Sarbanes-Oxley (the Corporate and Auditing Accountability, Responsibility, and Transparency Act of 2002), the SEC took on the additional responsibility of policing public company accounting, and reporting to Congress "the extent of off-balance-sheet transactions and the use of special purpose entities." A lot for one bunch of cops to do.

How many cops? Well, as of 2007, there were 5 commissioners and about 3,800 staff located in 19 offices around the country.[143] They covered more than 8,500 publicly traded companies listed on the New York Stock Exchange.[144] You do the math. This means, just for starters, that each staff member of the SEC would need to keep up with the quarterly reports, filings, accounting practices, and stock exchange activity of two companies. (Have you ever tried to thoroughly analyze just one quarterly report?)

But the review of corporate filing requirements is only one-quarter of the duties of the SEC. The organization also includes a Division of Market Regulation, overseeing the stock markets; a Division of Investment Management, responsible for the regulation of all investment management companies (wouldn't you like to have *that* job?); and the Division of Enforcement, the SEC cops on the beat who rush in and handcuff people when they spot flagrant violations of securities laws and regulations.[145]

Obviously, a few thousand people can't do all that, even if they skip their coffee breaks. But they can still be *expected* to do all that, and they can still be blamed for gross negligence of their oversight responsibilities when blatant infractions come to light. It was quite a spectacle, after the downfall of Bernie Madoff, to hear SEC chairman Christopher Cox deliver mea culpas for somehow failing to detect a multibillion-dollar Ponzi scheme.[146] "I am gravely concerned," Cox said in a written statement on December 16, 2008, "by the apparent multiple failures over at least a decade to thoroughly investigate these allegations or at any point to seek formal authority to pursue them. Moreover, a consequence of the failure to seek a formal order of investigation from the Commission is that subpoena power was not used to obtain information, but rather the staff relied upon information voluntarily produced by Mr. Madoff and his firm."

By then, of course, Harry Markopolos had documented his numerous attempts to bring the Ponzi scheme to light and get the SEC to take action. The watchdog agency had, without question, failed miserably to perform its mission. But . . . wait a minute. Are those 3,800 guys at the SEC the only thing standing between innocent investors and a $65 billion Ponzi scheme? What about all the banks that dealt with Bernie? What about the journalists who knew his hundreds of clients? What about the "sophisticated investors" who, supposedly, have developed twenty-first-century abilities to smell a rat? Let's not forget it was ultimately Bernie who blew the whistle on Bernie. All around him, in ever-expanding circles of sophisticated investors and expert traders and knowledgeable bankers and informed journalists, the whistles were notably silent. As for the SEC, it was just another whistle that failed to sound in the deafening silence.

Of course, the blame game is a merry one, and there's nothing more satisfying than hurling mud at a single target. So the employees of the SEC have taken a good drubbing. Lots of "shouldas" have been flying around. Shoulda seen the collapse of Bear Stearns a mile away. Shoulda caught all kinds of accounting irregularities in all kinds of companies, from the hallowed halls of General Electric to the sordid back rooms of WorldCom. Shoulda subpoenaed all kinds of people, rummaged around in computer files, recorded all kinds of conversations, and exposed all kinds of investor fraud. But wait . . . all of this with 3,800 guys, in 19 offices, watching over the ebb and flow of multitrillion-dollar dealings?

On September 29, 2009, a special investigative panel led by the SEC's inspector general, H. David Kotz, trotted back to Congress with a report on all the things the SEC needed to do to get its house in order.[147] Why not begin recording interviews with witnesses (something the SEC has not been doing)? Or, how about starting a database to keep track of tips and complaints (a novel idea, apparently)? There were a total of thirty-seven recommendations for improvements in the SEC's Inspections and Examinations Office, and another twenty-one recommendations for the Division of Enforcement. At the end of the report, Kotz sent those two SEC divisions off to do their homework, asking them to report back in forty-five days on how they would implement the recommendations of the investigative panel.[148]

In the melee following the Madoff scandal—coming so hard on the heels of the 2008 stock market crash—SEC commissioner

Christopher Cox came under considerable fire for committing a wide variety of sins. But he made some very interesting points about the limits of SEC oversight. The fact that investment banks could *voluntarily* "opt in" or "opt out" of oversight programs meant the SEC was at the mercy of Insider Arrogance. There was no way, he pointed out, that the SEC could "force large investment banks such as Goldman Sachs, Morgan Stanley, Merrill Lynch, Lehman Brothers, and Bear Stearns to report their capital, maintain liquidity or submit to leverage requirements."[149] As Cox so tactfully put it in a written statement, "The fact that investment bank holding companies could withdraw from this voluntary supervision at their discretion diminished the perceived mandate." Under the Gramm-Leach-Bliley Act—the one that caused Charles Glass to turn over in his grave—the SEC was given absolutely no authority.[150]

Indeed, it's a good point. How do you nab a drug dealer who has the option of saying, "Guys, I really appreciate your visit and your offer to inspect the premises, but sorry, not today." For all you know, he may be dealing in nothing more harmful than unadulterated Kool-Aid. But with that opt-out provision, you'll never know. It's a less-than-perfect policing system.

Under further pressure to explain how the SEC had failed to act to prevent market failure—and why—Cox suggested there were a couple more gaps in the agency's regulatory powers. He pointed out, for instance, that the entire market for credit default swaps was entirely unregulated. No disclosure necessary. The estimated exposure in that market, some $60 trillion, flowed through channels that were invisible to the naked eye. "Neither the SEC nor any regulator has authority even to require minimum disclosure," Cox noted.[151]

But what about the credit-rating agencies who continued to give triple-A ratings to public corporations that were teetering on the brink of insolvency? These were not even required to register with the SEC until September 2007. What followed was a ten-month investigation that led SEC regulators to conclude that the agencies had all kinds of conflicts of interest and irregularities. The SEC rule-making that ultimately passed Congress on December 3, 2008, would theoretically help to discipline these agencies. But, by then, the damage had been done.

The fact is, the SEC never stood a chance against the Masters of Insider Arrogance. Not a chance. Those 3,800 agents were outmanned, outflanked, and outwitted. Sure, they screwed up all over the place. But it takes more than a few chickens to guard a fox house.

A WHOLE NEW RULEBOOK

As I write, some 2,300 pages of new financial regulations have passed through Congress and received the signature of the president. They may, in fact, as Obama claims, "empower consumers and investors, bring the shadowy deals that caused this crisis into the light of day, and put a stop to taxpayer bailouts once and for all."[152] I wouldn't know. I'm only up to page twelve, and already my eyes are glazing over. But that's okay. These regulations weren't really written for you and me anyway. They were written for lawyers to read, and since the best-paid lawyers in the world are employed on Wall Street, you can be assured that in the days and months and years ahead, they will be prying meaning from every paragraph. So, too, will the regulatory agents who are meant to enforce those rules and maintain the American market as a clean, well-lit place.

Of courses, the lawyers from each side are working at cross-purposes. The Wall Street lawyers are out to find loopholes and weaknesses and contradictions where the rules can be challenged, edged around, or clambered over. The regulatory gang will be figuring out how they can slap wrists, arrest felons, and drag out testimony from the folks they need to interrogate in an attempt to get to the bottom of it all. And you can be assured the whole process will be further complicated, as it has been in the past, by regulators who get hired away to work for Wall Street firms, turning their expertise, for higher pay, toward interpreting those 2,300 pages more creatively than ever before.

Question is, will all this result in a place where investors can be honestly informed of what's really going on? Will the new regulations help them (and their money managers) decide where, and how, their money can best be used to support free enterprise and profit from legitimate returns on investment?

Investing in this market will always involve risk. That's just part of the equation. There will be no guarantees against the rise of a new Arrogance Cycle. But if we're going to keep this market as a place that people from all around the world will want to visit, I think we need to follow a few rules that are far simpler than those contained in 2,300 pages of turgid prose. They are the rules of a clean, well-lit place. For the sake of simplicity, let's call them Vince's Rules:

Rule #1: We get to inspect the dice.
Rule #2: We get to watch them roll.
Rule #3: We get to know who's betting.

That's it. Pretty simple.

Of course, following those rules isn't easy, and enforcing them is even harder—especially when we're competing against the powerful forces of Insider Arrogance.

CHAPTER 7

ARROGANT WATCHDOGS SLEEP

Your Arrogance Detectors

Spotting arrogance in others is relatively easy compared to seeing it in ourselves. Arrogance is like a lion in some stage of sleep or wakefulness. When roused, it begins pacing back and forth restlessly, growling, "Do something!" "Let's join in the feeding!" "Time to get in on the action." I've had clients who, after many years of prosperity, would begin to salivate at the rumor or the prospect of a sudden windfall. Someone is content, well fed, well housed, prepared for the future, with his or her wealth growing steadily. And then . . . what happens? They get a glimpse of sudden riches—the elusive prey. They hear the growls of other lions feeding. Suddenly all traces of caution are cast aside. As if seized by an uncontrollable fit of hunger, this cool, collected, and rational person I had known turns into an eager, insistent, famished hunter, leaving familiar territory to prowl the wilderness for a kill to satiate his appetite.

What are the signs? How do we anticipate that a surge of arrogance is about to rise up in you or me, and what can we do about it? As investors, we have to develop the skills to spot the warning signs. Why? Because one act of frenzied feeding can really screw us up in very expensive ways.

As far as I know, there's no 100 percent effective inoculation against arrogance. Arrogance is not an attractive trait; who among us wants to brand ourselves as the wise guy, the know-it-all, the smug bore who dominates conversations at the party? If you want to detect arrogance, I believe there are five warning signs that are definitely worth noticing. The first and most obvious is overspending; the second is a belief in secrets; third, falling in love with an idea; arrogant infallibility is fourth; and fifth, that horrible feeling that *you're being left behind.*

Let's have a look.

THE ARROGANCE OF OVERSPENDING

Chronic overindulgence in anything usually signals an attempt to compensate for some sense of inadequacy or insufficiency. The desperate need for more in hopes of satisfying the despondent feeling of emptiness—never having enough—drives many to destruction. *Retail therapy* is the humorous new idiom—the notion that you can make yourself feel better by shopping and spending. It works, too—for a while.

Whenever we look back on an Arrogance Cycle with the luxury of 20/20 hindsight, we're likely to experience schadenfreude (boy, did *they* get screwed!). It's pretty easy to beat up on others who showed egregious signs of greed and then got caught out. How is it possible, we wonder, that a single individual would require five homes or a private helicopter or a $20,000 shower curtain just to get along in the world? Why would a CEO whose every need is constantly being met with hosts of attendants, fleets of limousines, acres of property, and unlimited access to free food and drink and travel, feel the pressing need to double his or her salary, take out enormous loans against future income, or add yet another membership to the lists of exclusive clubs to which he/she belongs? When folks like that get their comeuppance, we love to hear the tales of their self-indulgence. Obviously, they were insanely insatiable.

But . . . not so fast. As I write, we are living in an era when the average ratio of debt obligations in American households is running around 13 percent of disposable income,[153] with the average personal savings rate, per household, hovering below 6 percent.[154] Ours is an era when the U.S. monthly balance of trade deficit is around $50 billion, largely because we consume more from sources around the world than we export to those places. Sure, we can blame some of that on the big, *big* spenders at the top of the heap, the 10 percent of our population that controls 80 to 90 percent of the wealth, including financial securities, business equity, and trust funds. (This 10 percent also owns 75 percent of the non-home real estate in the United States.[155]) But as wildly excessive as their habits may be, for *average* household debt to get that high, and savings to get that low, a lot of us must be doing what's called "living beyond our means."

Curious phrase, that. *Living beyond our means.* It sends a little tremor down the spine. Can we keep doing that? Grandpa and Grandma said we couldn't. Mom, Dad, harrumphing congress-people, and outraged editorial-page letter writers all agree, often truculently, that *we can't live beyond our means.* And then we go on, and the world doesn't come to an end, and we get stone-deaf to the clamor of that oft-repeated cliché of a warning.

If only we had a clue what we *mean* by "our means." Obviously, we don't. It's a moving target. A larger home with a bigger mortgage may be beyond your means today, but what if something were to change in the economic picture to assure you that a plethora of domestic square footage and property with more acreage is now *within* your means? Or what if you believe that your income will soon increase, and your circumstances will improve, and that a bigger house with more square footage and more acreage, though not quite within your means today, will be within your means tomorrow? Then "I Deserve It" kicks in, and before you know it, you're scanning real estate sections again. This is what I mean by a moving target. Our definitions of *within* and *beyond* (our means) are squishy. We live every day on the ill-defined borderland of what we need, what we deserve, what we can get, and how we can borrow to get what we believe can be ours.

It's a perfect place for arrogance to slip in. "Next year, I will get a nice promotion, and in two years my salary will be significantly more than it is today," is clearly an arrogant assumption. But that's exactly the assumption you'd *have* to be making if you took on an adjustable-rate mortgage. "I can't afford this new computer right now, but I'll figure out ways to pay for it by the end of the month" is not arrogant enough to be obnoxious, but just arrogant enough to become part of a personal trend to *buy now* on the assumption that you can *pay later*. Always, we are participants in the ongoing dance between optimism ("I *hope* I get a promotion and raise," "I *hope* I can make an end-of-the-month payment") and arrogance ("I *know* I will get a promotion and raise," "I *know* I can make an end-of-the-month payment"). There is a fine line between confident aspiration and entitled expectation, and the line is arrogance.

Perhaps there's an easy way to tell whether arrogance is winning out. You've got more home than you can afford. You've got bigger credit card bills than you can pay. Does that really mean you're arrogant? Or just hard up for the moment?

We run slam-bang into a contradiction when we try to screw our heads on straight and define the means within which we are supposed to live. Every force in the marketing and promotional universe is aimed toward making us believe that *the next big thing* that we undoubtedly deserve is within our means. Indeed, the classic measurements of economic growth involve two big factors—productivity and spending. Okay, it's a victory to be more productive, but where is the upside in increased spending (especially in the United States, where *consumer spending* makes all the difference)? Is this really a measure of prosperity, or if that spending is based on increased credit and reduced savings, is it an indicator of increased arrogance?

Moderate increases in consumption grow an economy. Consuming is the same as demanding. As demand increases, producers need to increase production. They need to hire more people and build larger factories to make enough stuff to meet demand. At a reasonable pace, those are great things for an economy and a society intent on improving its living standard.

The forces urging us to spend are powerful, overt, and relentless. The messages are on your computer, in magazines and newspapers, delivered on your TV screen, dumped in your mailbox. I'm not telling you anything you don't know, or that you aren't aware of. But even if we are inured to the onslaught of "buy" messages, almost to the point of immunity, I think it keeps feeding the part of the brain that says, "I Deserve It." It's not just the rich who deserve designer shoes, rare diamonds, Embraer jets, and Rolls-Royce Phantoms. You're just as deserving. Aren't you? You've worked just as hard. Maybe you're not quite as brilliant a financial strategist as the richest of the rich, but you're no less worthy of those rewards. So goes the thinking. That's when we click on the next item. We flip the glossy page. We absorb the ridiculous car commercial that shows yet another smooth-action, overpowered, sleek thing of beauty zooming over the landscape at three times the legal speed limit. "Not for me," we say. "Don't need it. Beyond my means." But then something inside goes snap or pop, and the advertising and marketing plant a kernel of need. (Believe me, it works; if it didn't, there would be no reason for advertisers to spend over $160 billion annually.[156])

With that snap and pop, the inner Arrogance Cycle begins. If you don't need that today, you file it away under "Maybe tomorrow." If you *can't* have that today, you file it away under "Someday I *can*." Even if you don't want it, the advertised item goes into a mental file of "other people do, and can, and will [want it, and have it]."

Once that starts to happen, it gets very hard to figure out what our "means" are. This is because there aren't any messages out there defining our means, while there are lots (and lots!) of messages telling us how to *live beyond* them.

When Everyone Wants in on "The Secret"

Another warning sign of the sneak-up of arrogance is the belief that somehow, somewhere, someone is holding on to the secret that will open the door to *your* personal prosperity and comfort. The trouble with that theory (or belief) is that it assumes external things will provide inner happiness and peace, and it puts way too much power into the hands of those who truly are arrogant.

During the upswing of any Arrogance Cycle, I find, more and more investors want to be "in" on the secrets. They look at the winners and say, "What aren't they telling me? What do *they* know that *I* don't know?" The reasoning goes like this: *The rich aren't rich because they work harder. It's because they know the magic formula. If I can just get my hands on the formula, I'll be rich, too.* Some experienced hands know better. But if you're just starting out as an investor—no matter what your preparation for market experience—you may be especially prone to this kind of thinking.

When I was a top salesperson at the investment firm, Alex. Brown & Sons, management liked to have me go around the country and breakfast with the young turks. The idea was, these young employees could ask questions, and they would get the benefit of whatever it was that was working for me. Time and again, I discovered that what they wanted to know was *the secret.* "How do you do it, Farr? How do you do it?"

I tried to explain. I kept track of how much I made in commissions over the previous year. Then I divided that number by how many hours I'd worked, so I knew how much I made every hour. Then I broke that down into fifteen-minute segments. My goal for the subsequent year was to increase my earnings by 20 percent. Applied to my workday, it meant that if I made $X dollars every fifteen minutes last year, I had to make $X + 20 percent this year. If I spent fifteen minutes gabbing with a friend during the day, then during the next quarter-hour I had to work twice as hard to make up for lost time. That was my secret. Set goals. Work to meet them. It was pretty grueling.

That wasn't what the guys around the breakfast table wanted to hear. They got really angry. "Don't BS us, Farr. That's not it. What's the *real* secret?" They didn't want to hear that it was hard work; they wanted to believe it was magic, and that if they just knew the proper incantation, they would be number one. The "hard work" message just made them feel bad about themselves.

Believing in secrets reinforces the arrogant mind-set. When profits begin surging, we begin to convince ourselves that we've *got* the secret! Secrets and magic provide us with the means to comfortably suspend disbelief and repress the nagging questions of common sense. Did I just make money on that tech stock? *Well, that's the secret; that's where all those other guys are making their money. I've got to find myself another dot-com to invest in.* Oil? I just made a profit in oil, and it's still going up. *The secret is oil! Forget the dot-coms; that's over. I'm going to get into oil.*

Wall Streeters call this "chasing the hot dot." It is spoken of disparagingly because it's always too late to follow once the dot is already hot. The real task is to do the dogged, diligent work that uncovers the dot before it warms up.

The contagion spreads in society, and pretty soon I have all the reinforcement I need. *I'm on to the secret—I'm among the elite.* And then, to convince myself, I back and fill, creating a logical-looking argument that explains how I discovered the secret.

Oil, in fact, is a good example of how this works. When oil went to $147.50 a barrel, I recall having discussions with a twenty-eight-year-old MBA who tried to explain to me why it had been obvious, all along, which direction oil was going. If I'd just been smart enough, two years before, I would have seen it clearly. All it took was research, logic, awareness. This is how he explained to me why the secret ("Oil can only go up") *should have been* so obvious to me: "Oil is a limited commodity which will be exhausted. Supply-demand, Farr. Limited supply. Rising demand. Get it?" *(Okay, I get that. But oil was in limited supply back in 1999 when the* Economist *announced we were drowning in oil and predicted the steady decline would continue until we hit $5 a barrel. Wasn't that the same commodity we're talking about today?)*

"Look, Farr, per capita use of oil in the U.S. has doubled in the last ten years. If people are using more, demand is going to skyrocket even higher." *(Yes, I get that; I really do. But that trend has been obvious for twenty years—a period when the price first declined to $10 a barrel and later rose to the neighborhood of $150 a barrel.)*

"But now it's a global market! China and India have become emerging markets with highly evolved societies that are using commodities at an outrageous rate." *(I get it! I get it! But you still haven't told me anything that hasn't been known for the last ten years, nor have you answered why the price of oil soared 47.5 percent in eighty-four days.)*

In truth, there was absolutely nothing wrong with his explanations. All the factors he mentioned had indeed contributed to the rise in oil prices; it helped to rationalize where we were. But it wasn't the whole story. And when Goldman Sachs, based on the obvious logic of these explanations, went ahead and predicted that the price of oil would go to $200 a barrel, it was clear that arrogance was out of control. Now the guys who had used the back-and-fill evidence to explain where we were (an innocent-enough process of rationalization) were using the same hollow evidence to predict where we would be (a dangerous belief in arrogant assumptions).

And, of course, oil never did hit $200 a barrel. Never even got close.

What my MBA friend was looking for, of course, was *the secret.* He wanted it in a nice, neat package, so he could search for the secret, find it, and then *own* it. As possessor of the secret, he would, of course, be a kind of guru, and the more he could get other people to believe that he held the keys, the higher he would rise on the elevator-chair of wisdom and know-how. It was all arrogance, of course. There was no secret, except hard work—the digging around to find out what works and what doesn't, what's true gold and what's fool's gold. If he found acolytes who would believe that he held the secret and the secret was oil, they would follow his venture into oil, and then he would be a god when oil was rising and a demon when it fell. As long as his acolytes maintained their belief in secrets, they would go searching again, find the prophet, follow the prophet, and the cycle would repeat. Believing in secrets only feeds the Arrogance Cycle . . . again and again and again.

THE ARROGANCE OF ABSOLUTE CERTAINTY

The MBA Who Believed in Oil is a perfect example of another kind of arrogance—the unshakable belief in a single idea. Ideas aren't bad. I have no problem with someone who takes on a new idea as a theory or proposition as grounds for fruitful discussion. I also don't have a problem with strong convictions. There was, for instance, a short period of time when it made perfect sense to invest in oil, and no doubt such opportunities will arise again. But I sense danger when an idea becomes fixed in someone's consciousness as *the* idea—the one and only, the solution to all problems and the answer to all prayers.

For a good sampling of what can happen when you get attached to the wrong idea, I sometimes ponder the example of Thomas Robert Malthus, widely regarded as the founder of modern economics. Malthus (1736–1834)[157] calculated the current world population and its rate of increase and compared it to the world food supply and its rate of increase. He made straight-line projections and determined that mankind would soon starve to death. Elaborating on this idea, and following it to what he considered a reasonable conclusion, Malthus suggested that allowing the poor to die from lack of medical care should therefore be considered a societal good. The Malthusian error was to assume that historical trends could be extrapolated without alteration or the introduction of new data.

It has always struck me as ironic that the seminal work of the first recognized economist was wrong. In retrospect, we can all be quite happy that Malthus did not find a quorum of followers who believed in his remarkable idea. Had he done so, you and I might not be here to discuss the pros and cons of it. In any case, it's a telling example of "great" ideas that can lead us astray, whether they arise from the brains of Malthus, or Alan Greenspan. Can you imagine believing so strongly in your own calculations and conclusions that you would declare a part of the population better off dead?! Stunning, no?

The longer I've stayed in this business, the more remarkable I find people who are entirely sure of themselves. People who have enormous certainty—with definite views of what's going on now, what it will mean, and what the implications are—are always kind of puzzling to me. It baffles me how they can be so sure, because the more I've experienced, the less sure I am about everything. For me, the learning cycle is a process of expanding one's universe to the point where you begin to grasp innumerable variables and get a keener understanding of the randomness of a lot of things.

Not the least of these variables is timing. Economists often can tell you which way the economy is going, but not when it will arrive there. When people come out and say, "I think this feels like a market top," I can appreciate that the idea makes sense to them, and I empathize with those feelings. But it's an opinion that is based on observation, nothing more, even if it comes from the lips of a business-news commentator or from the pages of a leading magazine. It's fine for someone to *say* something like that.

What bothers me is when they add, "Therefore, you should sell it." That's when I ask myself, "Why in God's name should I sell, based on this idea that someone else is selling me?" It's like asking someone else, "Should I marry Ethel?" and then deciding whether or not to marry Ethel on the basis of their answer.

Here's a reminder: *One way or the other, you're ignorant of something.* My friend Bobby O. provides a constant refresher in this concept. He's someone who has never been hemmed in by life's rules. His answer to almost any question or problem is, "Yes and no." "Do you believe this will happen?" I ask him. "Well, yes and no." "Would you do such-and-such?" "Yes, but on the other hand, no." (Bobby O.'s other life rule is "Admit nothing until you know what they know." But that's for another book.)

There is an important lesson in that response: Yes, it's great to have an idea, to look at things in a different way, to see possibilities. On the other hand, no idea is perfect. Following blindly is not the answer.

The president of one of the corporations I work with alleges there are only two types of people in our business—those who have been humbled, and those who are about to be. To that I would add, "Those not yet humbled are among the most arrogant on earth. Listen to their ideas, fine. But beware of following them." The voice in your head that says, "Well, yes . . . and no" is your best friend.

THE VOICE OF PRUDENCE

What does arrogance feel like? I doubt anyone can really answer that because arrogance is an emotion, and when you're caught up in an emotion, it's very difficult to recognize what's happening to you.

I am writing at a moment when my seventeen-year-old son is head over heels in love, and there's no talking to him about it. It's a madness; he's sort of "possessed." I know he's not going to snap out of it until this love thing has run its course. When someone falls in love, they're as hopeless as my seventeen-year-old kid. Head over heels, in the grip of a demonic possession. Ideally, someone would come along, slap this genius on the side of the head, saying, "Snap *out* of it!" But I can't do that with my son, and it wouldn't go down well if I tried it with one of these investors who is in the thrall of a great new idea and trembling with the awesomeness of what it may mean for their future. Arrogance soars, and he's listening to no one.

So . . . what's to be done? How can sanity be restored?

As you consider making a huge investment or life decision, go through the exercise of describing your plan out loud as if you were trying to explain it to a third party. Let's say, for example, you are planning to take absolutely everything—every last bit of cash you have, plus a home equity loan—and you're going to go out and buy gold coins. In the certainty of your own mind, you've searched your conscience, made a compelling argument, and decided that it holds up. This is absolutely, positively, without question, the right thing for you to do. (Remember: You are in the grip of an emotion.)

The first step is to articulate your decision and the reasoning that lies behind it. I recommend doing that out loud. Okay, you've made this decision to buy a truckload of gold coins. Now, figure out how you'd explain this decision to a business school class or a group of investment professionals.

Another tactic: Talk to a friend. Explain what you're doing, and why. Write it down on paper if you have to. (Incidentally, this is something I'd advise doing any time you're making a shift of more than 20 percent in your investment plan or planning to move more than 20 percent of your assets.)

If you can't imagine talking to a business school class, and you don't have a friend who's particularly interested in your investment decisions, then I advocate "the prudent man rule." Sophisticated investors always talk about this rule. Go through the exercise of asking yourself: What would a prudent man in a similar situation, with similar information, actually do? Ask yourself, "What would he warn me about? What advice would he give me?" Then listen . . . very carefully.

My version of the prudent man rule is "What would my dad say?" My dad ran the money in our house, and I think he was always overly cautious. Given any situation that had a silver lining, he could always find a cloud. Did I love the sound of that critical voice? Not usually. But that critical voice, at times, can be helpful. So I still listen. When I feel my enthusiasm start to run away with itself, I try, "What would Dad say?" It's not a bad way to improve financial decision-making.

As you're going through this process, be sure to ask the hard questions—and a lot of them. You may have complete faith in your gold-coin investment, but is that faith built on reason or emotion? If it's strong enough to endure, your faith will stand up to questioning. Think about the people you respect and the sorts of questions they would ask you. Then prepare for the interview. (That will help you learn more about your investments.) Ask yourself:

- Why do I feel I should be investing this capital right now? Am I sure I won't need this money? Can I tie up this money for a few years without needing it to fund my living expenses?

- Is this a risk that's appropriate for me? Can I *afford* to lose this money?

- Do I need to risk losing this money (in gold coins or anything else)? If I remain on a safe course with my money, can I still accomplish my investment goals?

If you're being swept up in a tide of emotion for this gold-coin investment, the natural emotional response is pure enthusiasm. The prospect of profits does that to us. What if you have a prospect of doubling your money? Tripling your money? Isn't that worth looking at?

Perhaps, but first you have to ask yourself, "What for? What am I trying to gain? What do I want my money to do?"

Okay, so let's say it makes sense to take bigger risks than you're taking at the present time. Then the next set of questions is all about the investment you want to make. For instance:

- Does this company have a lot of cash? A lot of debt? What sort of money are they earning?

- What sort of moat is protecting their business? How high are the barriers to entry? What differentiates them from potential competition?

- Do they have proprietary technology, and do they have a legal department that's able to defend their proprietary resources? Is it a technology that can be modified with something new that, in turn, can be protected with new patents?

- How much of the market do they already have—and how much can they really grow?

- What's their tax situation?

- What's their management look like? How long has it been in place, and have they managed through ups and downs of market and economic cycles?

- Where do the threats come from? Are there big lawsuits out there? Is another company developing new technology that could make the current technology (of your investment target) obsolete?

These are boring questions. They're the ones that slow you down, make you look again and dig deeper. These are the kinds of questions that will make you doubt your absolute faith in the moves you want to make—and they should. Whether your passion is gold coins, or something more esoteric, it's useful to remember that you really are in the throes of an emotional state. You're in love, and love breeds arrogance. It's a treacherous place to be.

ARE YOU FEELING LEFT BEHIND?

My grandfather used to tell me a story about a little kid who's sitting on the curb crying, and along comes an old man and asks him why he's crying. The little kid looks up with tearful eyes and says, "'Cause I can't do what the big boys do."

The old man tries to think of something to say to console the boy but can't come up with anything. Finally, he just sits down on the curb next to the little boy, puts his face in his hands, and starts crying, too.

My grandfather didn't have to explain. I got it. Young or old, naive or wise, all of us throughout our lives want to play with the big boys. And if we can't actually do it, we want to be perceived as doing it.

Dwell on that long enough, and it'll make you sad. It'll make you weep. But, it's still something we try for, and it gets us in all kinds of trouble.

In the frenzy of an Arrogance Cycle, everyone wants to do what the big boys are doing because the big boys are making money. They're raking in huge bonuses—and something more: They've cut themselves loose from mundane concerns. They've shrugged off the caution and reserve that are shared by the rest of us. The big boys are big because they *think big,* and when you think big, you're creative, you're innovative, you're at the top of your game. For instance, you can look at a bundle of worthless assets and think to yourself, "Well, these assets are worthless, I know that, but not everyone knows that. What if I can hide that fact from a great number of people and, instead of mentioning these assets' worthlessness, I say that they are really quite valuable? In fact, I'll put a *big number* on these assets, and I'll get some other big guys to attest to their value, and since everyone wants to play with the big guys, they'll say, 'Hey, look—these guys have something that they all agree is of great value.' And if we can do that, then the guys who are not big guys, but who want to play with the big guys, will *believe us*." Never forget how Tom Sawyer talked the other kids into painting his fence.

In 2008, after oil went through the roof, a client whom I'll call Chester Wilson gave me a call. He wanted to talk about what was happening and what he should do with his money. At age sixty-three, he had a $3 million portfolio, but that wasn't enough. He didn't feel like he was playing with the big guys. He wasn't participating in the then-current bubble, and he was feeling scared, angry, and out of control. When we met and reviewed his portfolio, he attacked us and discounted the data we had produced. "The world has changed," he said. "You're not keeping up." Oil was $145 per barrel. He fired us and went with a manager in New York. Two years away from retirement, and he wanted to get into the heart of the game and become a real player! Most of all, he didn't want to be left behind, so he invested 90 percent of his assets in oil and energy shares as they peaked. Sadly, Chester is way behind now, and may never get back to even.

There is always that feeling that the world has changed, and if you're stuck with the old metrics, you'll be left behind. But how can you make smart choices about something that you don't understand? As Warren Buffett said, "If I don't get it, I'm not going to own it."

The most important facet of investing is *understanding what you need your money to do.* When someone comes in to me and says,

"I want to buy . . . hog futures," I ask, "Why? What for? What are you trying to gain? What is it you would like your money to do?"

If the answer is, "Other people are making money there," that's not good enough. I want to know how much you need for yourself, today; how much for your children; how much to prepare for the future. If you're not covered in those areas, then let's come up with a plan to get a reasonable return on your investments and make them grow. But let's not get into hog futures unless you know what they're all about.

You don't need the textbook plan. You don't need to beat your brother-in-law who has just bought a biotech and is rubbing your nose in it every time the stock takes a jump. You just need to make sure you're going to be okay financially when you need to be. When should you be satisfied? When you know that, at any point in your life, should the music stop, you'll absolutely have a chair.

YOUR PERSONAL ARROGANCE SCALE

Given the humiliating setbacks that many investors have experienced (and felt in their solar plexuses) during the first decade of this millennium, it might be hard to believe that arrogance will ever reign supreme again. But let's guess otherwise. It will. The cycle can move swiftly, rising at a frenzied pace with the next big bubble. And because of the infectious nature of arrogance, the virus may already be nested inside you, just waiting to give you a fever when enthusiasm outruns reason.

With this danger in mind, I've developed a very straightforward self-evaluation to help clients keep tabs on their own personal arrogance factors. There are six questions in this survey, and it takes just a few moments to complete and score. You can take it online at www.arrogancecycle.com and quickly weigh your personal results against an overall arrogance scale for all respondents. Or try it here.

SURVEY: WHAT'S YOUR INVESTING EGOTYPE?

For each of the following questions, circle one answer on the scale from 1 to 5. Circle 1 for *strongly disagree,* circle 5 for *strongly agree,* or choose a rating from 2 to 4 if you're somewhere in between. When you're done, add up your answers for a total score.

I am an aggressive investor.

1   2   3   4   5

I believe I can predict and navigate the market better than others.

1   2   3   4   5

Most of my losses in investing have been due to market and other conditions beyond my control.

1   2   3   4   5

I expect to make more money than others over time.

1   2   3   4   5

I believe that others will follow my advice in investing.

1   2   3   4   5

I do not value the opinions and insights of market experts.

1   2   3   4   5

TOTAL: _____

What kind of investor are you? Your scoring on this Arrogance Scale survey will help you see where you stand.

What should you do with the results?

The purpose of this survey is to help you determine for yourself where you rank on the arrogance scale. The goal is *not* to change your personality but simply to help you recognize where you may be most vulnerable in making investment decisions. What I'm about to describe are certainly stereotypes, and by definition, it's risky to stereotype anyone. But sometimes it can be extremely helpful to recognize those aspects of our personality (especially the arrogant ones) that can lead us astray. There are elements of these descriptions that you may recognize, and other aspects that you may reject as "not being me." But it's important to see your rating on the arrogance scale so you can evaluate your day-to-day decision-making.

This self-evaluation will give you a quick and objective view of your investing egotype.

SCORE 20–30: THE ARROGANT INVESTOR

If your ranking on the arrogance scale is 20–30, let's just say your self-confidence, when it comes to investing, is in the range of *very confident* to *hyper-self-confident*. You're definitely high on the arrogance scale. Obviously we all have some tendencies to become arrogant. If all is well with our egos, we're likely to have a sustained belief in our ability to understand and manage difficult situations, to make our way in the world, to reach sound judgments, and to take care of those who need to be taken care of. But the truly Arrogant Investor poses a risk not only to himself or herself, but to others as well. Why? Because he's *right*. Not sometimes. Not provisionally. But always. Unquestionably. Right.

Profits, as I have pointed out, feed arrogance, especially when profits come quickly. That's a hardwired response, and it's as unconscious as the response of a small rodent in the lab that gets a food pellet every time it makes the "right" choice. The small rodent pushes the lever, the pellet is delivered, and something Darwinian inside a rat-size brain signals, "Do it again and you'll get food again." Well, same here—except in the human brain, that signal is more like "I got it right." The "I" makes all the difference. Somewhere within that "I" who got it right is a person whom we flatter as being prescient, clever, and fast-acting. Really, when you think about it, a *quite remarkable person* got it right. And if that quick and sagacious person *gets it right* several times in a row, after a while we begin to think very highly of him and his judgment. Welcome to the dawning of arrogance.

If there seems to be an aura of religious belief around this transformation, I think the analogy is not far off. In my experience, "believers" do indeed have a certain aura of fundamentalism about them. They cling to a newfound religion of profits (delivery of the food pellet) with remarkable tenacity. They reject anything that is not in the book of common belief (in what creates the profits), and they reject anyone who isn't a true believer. Hard questions are regarded as threatening because Arrogant Investors understand, at some level, the fragility of their belief system, and realize that if they were to give quarter to doubt, the magic would fail.

(I'm reminded of the scene in *Peter Pan* when Tinker Bell looks like she must be dying, and Peter Pan comes out and says, "You have to *believe* in Tinker Bell if she's going to live." Sure enough, everyone begins to clap and cheer and proclaim their love for Tinker Bell. It works: Tinker Bell rises from the floor. But what if someone had questioned whether Tinker Bell was really real? This is the fear of doubt and skepticism that sows dread in the heart of any true believer. But Peter Pan knows us and plays to our thirst for magic and hunger for secrets.)

At the highest end of the scale of arrogance, you are willing to put all of your money in what you believe in. (Makes sense, in that frame of reference: If you weren't willing to gamble everything on what you believe in, then you're not really a believer after all—are you?)

A client of mine, I'll call him Steve, came to me at the height of the oil boom—when the prices of oil and gas took off—and he said, "Michael, I know what I'm doing now." And when I asked what he was going to do, he said the magic words, "Oil-well partnerships."

I knew about oil-well partnerships. They are very complicated. You buy a share in a putative oil field, and it may or may not turn out to have oil. If it does, you move into another layer of investment. If the field is dry, you realize losses that can be used for tax relief. Steve caught the last five years of the oil boom. He moved tens of millions of dollars into that sector. A couple of years before it went bust, he informed me that I needed to unload everything I had and join him in these limited partnerships. It was the new way of the world. Steve's story is painful not only because he's a dear friend who lost his shirt, but also because he kicks himself mercilessly for being so stupid. Not "stupid," Steve. Arrogant.

In a nutshell, that's the mantra of the Arrogant Investor. It is the expressed belief of a person who knows—*knows!*—there is some permanent change taking place in the market. In his or her view, the inexorable trend can only lead one way, and those who are sharp-eyed enough to detect the trend will be the winners, and those who fail to subscribe to the new belief will be the losers.

A stereotype? Yes. But within each of us are the seeds of this level of arrogance.

SCORE 13–19: THE EGOBALANCED INVESTOR

If you're within this range on the Arrogance Index, I suspect you have a sufficient amount of measured skepticism to counterbalance ardent belief.

I went to Gonzaga College High School in Washington, D.C. The Jesuits who taught us were great fans of questions. The priests posited that one's faith had to be strong enough to question. It strikes me as sound investment advice to subject your beliefs to ongoing questions.

It is always a pleasure to work with people who are able to handle these kinds of questions without flinching. Certain clients immediately come to mind—one couple in particular. Dave Morton is a professor, and Karen is a lawyer. As they've been raising their children, they've saved money regularly, putting aside 15 percent every month as regularly as they pay any other bill. They've paid off their home and increased their savings. They have a planned approach to their investments. They look at the long term. They diversify. They understand risk and volatility. While they don't like bear markets (who does?), they expect them, and live through them, with abiding optimism that everything is going to be okay over time and in the end. They don't fret over prices every day, they don't expect to make a gazillion dollars, and when the market goes south, they don't think the world is going to end.

Dave and Karen also know why they're putting money in the market in the first place. They have reasonable confidence in it, and measured optimism, and they expect that their investments will grow and accumulate to provide them the comforts they desire in their old age. They talk about their investment decisions openly, between them, so there are no secrets. Both are responsible—and equally to blame or credit—for gains and losses.

They work with me, and I look forward to their calls. They work with other investment advisors, too, and that's fine. I look forward to every meeting with them and every well-thought-out decision they make.

Egobalance? The Mortons exemplify it. Are they in it for themselves and their family? Absolutely—that's where the ego comes in. But this is self-interest, not selfishness. There's rationality to everything the Mortons do—a measured purpose. They don't take on the gambler's mentality ("Today's my lucky day!"). They don't resort to market-hater's remorse ("Everything's turned to crap! I'm screwed!").

So—what was your range on the Arrogance Index? I guess my bias is perfectly clear. This is the range where you *want* to be—in the range of egobalance.

SCORE 6–12: THE EGOPHOBIC INVESTOR

A number of different factors create insecurity in investors. First of all, inexperience; second, a bad experience (or a number of them); and third, I've found that family history, in very interesting ways, can have an indirect but very important effect on investor confidence.

If you scored in the 6–12 range on the arrogance scale, it's no reflection on your personal sense of self-worth, but in all likelihood, it does translate into behavioral patterns that will have a direct impact on your investment decisions. The inexperienced investor, for instance, can suffer from analysis paralysis. He or she wants to know everything there is to learn about a company's history, its P&Ls dating back dozens of years, its past market performance, etc. That's healthy curiosity. Getting answers to questions like that will contribute to sound decision-making. No argument there. But when it becomes apparent that no amount of additional information can possibly enhance the quality of a decision, I suspect there are other reasons for not acting. Could it be fear of the market itself? Could it be fear of making a mistake, or of losing money? Whatever their source, aggregate fears impede action, and the egophobic investor may end up walking away rather than taking any risk at all.

(One sure signal of analysis paralysis is when a client asks me where a company that I've recommended *is located*. At that point, I know we've come to the end of relevant questioning as far as their decision-making is concerned. What possible difference could it make where a company is located? Are they going to choose a company located in Nevada and spurn one located in Massachusetts on the basis of local geography and customs?)

This kind of paralysis is not exclusively the domain of newcomers, however. Experienced investors may be just as prone to putting on the brakes when they're suffering in the aftermath of significant losses. It's the downside of the Arrogance Cycle. Previously, their profits sent their arrogance soaring. When profits disappear, disappointment sets in. As the pendulum swings, the doubts become as great as their prior beliefs.

These lows are just as debilitating to judgment as the arrogance highs. The humble frame of mind leads to excessive self-doubt. Solid facts and figures are questioned. It's a tremulous state of mind, and unless the egophobic investor begins to move up the scale to egobalance, he or she is quite likely to go through the cycle all over again the next time they're caught up in a bubble.

Another type of egophobic investor is the person whose steps are dogged by family or personal history. I had a client several years ago who realized steady income from a sound investment strategy. As yields fell, I shocked her when I suggested that she use some of her capital gains to supplement her income. This is known as total return investing. Her father, she said, had cautioned her that she should never—but *never!*—touch the principal. Her father had died many years before, but those words still had power. As we worked out, on paper, what percentage she could draw down from capital for the greatest tax advantage and the maximum returns, she acknowledged the soundness of the approach. It all made sense and was rational. Nonetheless, she was truly very upset, embarrassed—and scared. "I can't imagine what my father would say if he saw me doing this!"

Another client of mine, Ralph, had a net worth close to $37 million when he sold his business. Obviously, he had some decisions to make about what he was going to do with that money. But he froze. What bothered him most, as it turned out, was nothing in his own experience, but rather the memory of *his* own father—who had passed away *thirty years before*—whom he described as "a blue-collar worker who never made more than $22,000 a year." As Ralph thought about putting $100,000 in a stock I was recommending, and another hundred grand over there, he kept saying things like, "My father would kill me if he saw how I was throwing this money around." "Well," I responded, "I don't think that's too likely, since he's been dead thirty years. But the fact is, you've got $37 million in your account, and you need to make some decisions about what to do with it."

YOUR EGO AND THE MARKET

It's a mistake to confuse selfishness with self-interest. It feels more and more like both share negative connotations, but they are really quite different. Adam Smith in *Wealth of Nations* argued that three things were required in order to have a successful economy: free trade, division of labor, and pursuit of self-interest. Market prices are based on the pursuit and defense of one's interests. *Fair value* is defined as the price at which a seller who is willing, but not obliged, to sell, sells to a buyer who is willing, but not obliged, to buy. It is presumed that both buyer and seller know what they're doing, and why, and that they will somehow be better off for doing it.

At its core, this is a free market, and free markets are efficient and work best. If you're participating in it as an investor, you're taking risks in a marketplace that is ruled by no higher law than the universal desire to realize profits. No amount of oversight can rein in that overwhelming desire, because it's fundamental to the way markets work. If there's someplace in this crowded marketplace for a new vendor with a new kind of product, then, guess what—that vendor is going to appear, even when there's still rubble left over from the last little quake that rippled through the market.

The incontrovertible truth is that any time you make an investment, you're making a guess. You hope it's an educated guess, but still, it's a guess. Results will either verify or nullify the soundness of your judgment, but please don't forget that you're guessing. Please don't say that you *know*. That's a big mistake. We *don't* know. And if we convince ourselves we're *not* guessing, that we really have powers of prescience that no one else possesses—well, that's just arrogance, and it's profoundly dangerous.

Being aware of your own egotype will help you decide, personally, how much you need to compensate for arrogance. Yes, there are rules and regulations that help govern U.S. markets, but it's clear from history that you can't assume the SEC or Moody's will play the role of watchdog for you. You're the watchdog. Only you. Which is why it doesn't pay for you to get caught up in the Arrogance Cycle. An arrogant watchdog is one that sleeps.

In a free and open market, there will always be a certain amount of uncertainty. The challenge is to figure out how much uncertainty you can tolerate. If the answer is zero—if you won't invest in anything unless you're 100 percent certain that it's the right thing to do—then (ironically) you're at the greatest risk of all. Because the belief that you know, for sure, what's going to happen next is an illusion; that belief itself is a petri dish for the growth of arrogance.

You can't be certain. What you *can* do is make educated guesses based on the information that's available to you. If we can make sure that information is right, you'll be better off. But finding the right information is never easy, particularly when the Arrogance Cycle is in a big market-wide upswing.

There are some good ways to tell when that's happening, or about to happen, as we'll see in the next chapter.

CHAPTER 8

RUNAWAY ARROGANCE

AND THE BUBBLE MACHINE

The Quality of Arrogance Is Not Strained

If the ultra-arrogant were sequestered in their own casino where they could make (and break) the rules, society would be a lot safer. Unfortunately, as we know, that's not the case. As we have seen, they often have the power to create the kinds of bubbles and manias that lead, inevitably, to crashes and panics. And, as we have also seen, their power comes not just from the ability to act but also their power to influence—to create, essentially, a viral epidemic of arrogance that spreads through society, catching the wary and unwary alike, sweeping aside all doubts and objections, and ultimately leaving a path of destruction in their wake.

What contributes to these cycles? It must be obvious that the arrogant are always among us. Their behavior may be reined in by circumstances, by limitations of means, by rules or laws or regulations, but because they appeal to tendencies and needs that are in all of us, their potential influence is widespread. Why, then, do we see times when the arrogance factor prevails and other periods when it is calmed, restrained, or hidden? Can we see these cycles coming? Can we anticipate them in some way—and, if that's not quite possible, can we sharpen our own powers of observation so we know *it's happening again* and take some measures to protect ourselves and our investments? In sum, what is the correlation between the rise in the "arrogance factor" and speculative bubbles that occur in the stock, real estate, or tulip bulb markets?

These were some of the questions I began discussing with my colleagues at Farr, Miller & Washington and with other professionals from other disciplines. Given our experience working with investors and dealing with several decades of market fluctuations, we all have a feel for the tidal rise and fall of arrogance. When arrogance was rising, we would begin to hear phrases uncannily similar to those of winning gamblers—"can't lose," "will only go up," "sure thing." (On the downswing, we became accustomed to hearing more despondent strains of "I was an idiot," "I should have known," and, most despairing of all, "I'm so screwed.") If we could collate and quantify the exuberant refrains when the tide of arrogance was rising, I believed we could construct a model that would signal all of us to be on the alert for the coming bubble. Unfortunately, it's impossible to measure the frequency of arrogant utterances.

What about the things we *can* measure? Which ones, we asked, are strong indicators of a rising arrogance factor? Could we, in fact, see indices that would correlate with, say, the Dow Jones Industrial Average?

A STOCK MARKET STUDY

First we took the long view. We considered episodes of boom and bust dating from the beginning of the twentieth century to the present day. The data for this period are good. The stock market, though transformed in many ways by changes in regulations and technology, has provided a consistent measure of commerce and investment activity. And we have enough boom-bust cycles within that period to determine whether there were good, fair, or poor correlations with arrogance indices.

Our objective, then, was to create a quantifiable measurement of arrogance. Could it be done? We found a number of factors that stood out. Among them:

- *Savings rates.* How much personal income is kept in savings, in liquid assets, or, for that matter, in cash under the mattress? Over the years there have been wide fluctuations in savings rates for a variety of reasons. Of course, when times are hard, people have to dig into savings, and like it or not, the personal savings rate declines. But there can be other reasons. One is cultural. (In Japan, for instance, the personal savings rate—in good times and bad—is generally much higher than in the United States.) Another factor is the accessibility of credit. (If we think we can readily get a loan to tide us over through lean times, then we have less incentive to sock away something for a rainy day.) And, surely, another important factor is arrogance. If we get so full of ourselves and confident of our choices that we figure there won't be any more rainy days, then why bother stashing away extra cash that we could otherwise use for immediate gratification? Could it be that a rising Arrogance Cycle would correspond to a decline in personal savings?[158]

- *Asset prices.* In the midst of an Arrogance Cycle, it is evident that people will put prices on goods, real estate, commodities, or securities that far exceed the present value of the asset's future cash flows. Investing in tulips may seem foolhardy, but not if you're in the midst of a mania for tulip investment. Given an overabundance of enthusiasm, people will perceive value in South Sea properties that they've never even visited, in railroad lines that lead nowhere, in land that is overgrown with weeds or crawling with alligators. We've seen investors pour money into stocks of companies that trumpet their own value, in ephemeral concepts of companies that do not yet exist, in companies that make a business of buying and selling other companies. Sometimes the only value is a promise. Literally anything can be inflated in value when an Arrogance Cycle is going full tilt. True, some of these investments make sense. Others, so removed from reality that they seem laughable, don't. It seems obvious that when stocks are wildly overinflated (as measured by price/earnings ratios), there's reason for investor caution.

We looked at historical prices for a wide variety of assets. For housing prices, we tracked the Case-Shiller U.S. National Home Price Index, which provides quarterly data on home prices.[159] We also tracked a variety of commodity prices, including gold and oil. And finally, we looked at historical price-to-earnings multiples on the U.S. stock market.

- *Income concentration.* Though the market is always crowded with eager investors, and many more are clamoring to become part of the club, when there is a rising Arrogance Cycle, income tends to become more concentrated. Greater riches flow into the hands of ever-fewer individuals who profit disproportionately from speculative fervor.[160]

- *Luxury spending.* In each era, and therefore in each cycle, the definition of "luxury" is in the eye of the beholder. Even so, we wondered whether there was some way to analyze the way people were spending their money—that is, whether there was a distinct shift toward spending on luxury goods during an Arrogance Cycle. Could we define, first of all, what were "luxury goods" or "luxury stocks," and then measure the uptick in spending on luxury goods? Or was the whole definition of "luxury" too subjective to work with?

In an attempt to track luxury goods spending trends, we analyzed a basket of ten companies that sell "luxury" items. We tracked the stock prices and earnings at these ten companies over the past twenty years. The companies were Rolls-Royce Group, LVMH Moet Hennessy Louis Vuitton, Empresa Brasileira de Aeronautica, Sotheby's, Tiffany & Co.,

Daimler AG, Diageo PLC, Coach, Inc., Saks, Inc., and Royal Caribbean Cruises.

- *Consumer confidence.* The Consumer Confidence Index is an interesting measurement of how people feel about their financial situations and what they regard as prospects for the future. It's probably the best measurement we have to figure out whether the mood about the economy is generally optimistic, pessimistic, or neutral. But what happens to consumer confidence, we wondered, when arrogance is running high? Confidence is all well and good, but when it tips over into *over*confidence—when people have fantasies about how well they are doing and about their future prospects—wouldn't that be a sign of a surging Arrogance Cycle?[161]

- *Credit supply.* Though difficult to define and track, we thought some measure of credit availability would be extremely helpful in signaling arrogance. After all, we need not look too far back into history to uncover the true cause of the most recent economic decline. An overabundance of credit, sparked largely by a surge in home prices, made consumers all over the country feel rich. Given easy access to their home equity, homeowners tapped this paper wealth in droves to buy whatever their hearts desired. Even those homeowners who did not take out home equity loans felt much more comfortable spending freely with the knowledge that the gains on their homes would serve as nice retirement nest eggs. As home prices rose, savings rates declined, credit card balances increased, and caution was thrown to the wind.

  In an effort to measure the supply of credit to consumers we considered several potential metrics. We looked at historical credit card mail solicitation volumes and response rates.[162] We looked at the Federal Reserve Board's Senior Loan Officer Opinion Survey, which tracks demand for loans and bank lending standards.[163] And finally, we looked at the year-over-year growth in consumer credit, which includes credit cards and auto and installment loans (excluding loans secured by real estate).[164]

The next challenge: to figure out which of these measurable factors correlate with cycles of boom and bust in the stock market. We focused on what's been going on during the past twenty years. Our methodology was to perform regression analysis using the many different "independent" variables described above to predict the "dependent" variable, which is the S&P 500. In testing the many different metrics, we found varying degrees of correlation with stocks. While most had some predictive value, some did not. And some of the variables were highly correlated to each other, a situation called "multicollinearity," which leads to weaker regression results.

In the end, we identified three factors as the most reliable indicators of arrogance in the market:

1. Personal savings rate;
2. Income concentration; and
3. Consumer confidence.

Using the Standard & Poor's index as a measurement of stock performance, we found that these three factors could explain 90 percent of the variability in the S&P 500 over the past twenty years, with an increase in stocks associated with a decline in the personal savings rate, an increased concentration of income in the top 1 percent of the population, and a rise in consumer confidence.

ARROGANCE FACTOR #1: PERSONAL SAVINGS RATE

By definition, the personal savings rate (PSR) is expressed as a percentage of the population's disposable income.[165] To calculate this ratio, the Bureau of Economic Analysis first looks at disposable personal income (for each family), then subtracts expenditures (including interest payments but not mortgage payments) and taxes to arrive at a figure for "savings." That's the numerator. The denominator is disposable personal income.[166] So if you save $4,000 and make $100,000 in a year, your personal savings rate is 4 percent.

As you can see in the chart below, the PSR was hovering around 6 and 7 percent in the early 1990s when the S&P Index was in the range of 300 to 600. As the market gathered momentum, personal savings took a nosedive. By September 2000, when the S&P was over 1,400, personal savings had fallen to 3.1 percent. As the market bottomed out in 2002 and began a meteoric rise over the next five years, personal savings did not rise above 3 percent. And in September 2007, with the bubble at its peak and the S&P peaking at 1527, the personal savings rate scraped bottom—1.8 percent of disposable income. We were essentially emptying our pockets as we enjoyed the thrill of a joyride through false prosperity.

S&P 500 and Savings/DPI [167]

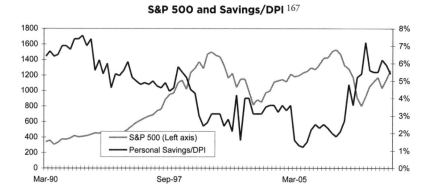

ARROGANCE FACTOR #2: CONCENTRATION OF INCOME
When relatively few individuals at the top of the heap receive a vast share of income, it's another indicator of market arrogance.

The top 1 percent of the U.S. income bracket has earned more than 20 percent of the pretax income just three times in the last 100 years—in 1928, 2000, and 2005. All three times, the peaks were followed by market crashes. The graph below tracks the percentage of income earned by the top 1 percent between 1913 and 2008.

Top 1 Percent Share of Total Pretax Income, 1913–2008 [168]

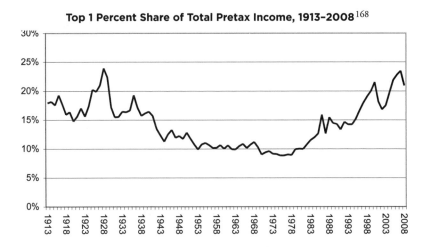

Of course, when 1 percent of the population receives one out of every five dollars—and the remaining 99 percent of the population has to live off the other four—there are all kinds of ramifications. That elite 1 percent gets an ever-greater sense of feeling bulletproof. They are immune to the needs that afflict other members of society.

Moreover, history has shown that extreme financial disparity coincides with market bubbles. Though the GDP may be growing, the majority of the population is not receiving the benefits of that growth. The top 1 percent, the super-affluent, has huge reserves of disposable income, while many of the earnings-starved 99 percent are not benefiting to nearly the same extent from economic growth.

In the years from 1990 to 2010, I believe we have become more acutely aware of these discrepancies. But they are not unprecedented. From 1927 to 1937, both the percentage of income and the S&P 500 index were volatile. As you can see from the graph below, between 1927 and 1937, every time the percentage of income pushed above or close to 20 percent (it was at 19.29 in 1936), the S&P 500 index proceeded to post a major decline. In 1928, both the S&P 500 and the percentage-of-wealth index had reached all-time highs, at 24.4 and 23.9, respectively. The S&P does not return to this level until 1952 (measured on a year-ending basis), thus suggesting that stock values were wildly overinflated in 1928.

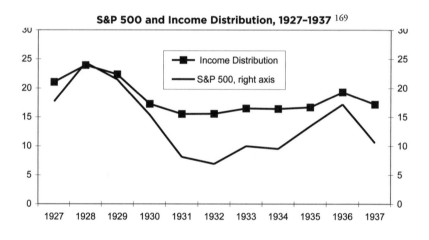

S&P 500 and Income Distribution, 1927–1937 [169]

From 1974 to 1984, the percentage of income earned by the top 1 percent was at an all-time low, and during that time, the S&P 500 index shows a period of steady growth. In fact, the S&P swelled from 68.56 to 167.24, a growth rate of about 144 percent, while the income earned by the top 1 percent remained between 9.12 percent and 11.99 percent. The graph on the next page shows how a period of more evenly distributed income appears to lead to periods of long-term steady growth for the S&P 500.

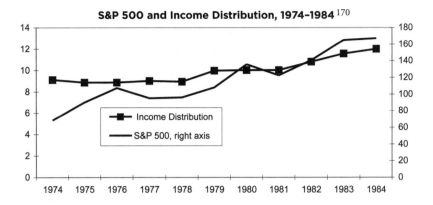

S&P 500 and Income Distribution, 1974–1984 [170]

Another extremely volatile period for both economic measures occurred between 1996 and 2006. As you can see from the next graph, any time the percentage of income pushed above 20 percent, there was a steep decline in the S&P 500 in the subsequent years. In the years 1999 and 2000, the percentage of income earned by the top 1 percent of the population was 20.04 percent and 21.52 percent, respectively. From year-end 2000 to year-end 2001, the S&P fell 172.2 points, or over 13 percent.

The percentage-of-income index pushed above 20 again in 2005.

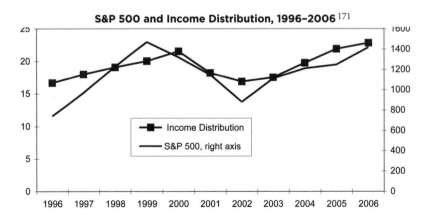

S&P 500 and Income Distribution, 1996–2006 [171]

As the market clambered to even giddier heights in 2007, the concentration of income in the top 1 percent reached above 23 percent—as might be predicted, since it is the wealthiest segment of the population that owns the greatest share of investments, and therefore gets the most benefit from a bubble. It's remarkable, however, that through the crash of 2008, followed by recession, more than 20 percent of income was still going to 1 percent of the population.

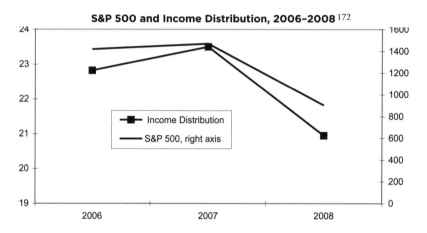

S&P 500 and Income Distribution, 2006–2008 [172]

There seems to be a desire to place some moral judgment on these statistics; please note that we are not. We can't imagine how one might determine the proper number of rich, poor, or otherwise. We will leave that to our friend Malthus and his like. It strikes us that less-concentrated income levels add breadth to economic demand at all income strata, and this, we believe, is what drives the corresponding periods of economic and market strength. Suffice it to say that for our purposes, market froth (and therefore arrogance) appears most glaring when we get to the extreme scenario whereby 1 percent of the population earns over 20 percent of pretax income.

ARROGANCE FACTOR #3: CONSUMER CONFIDENCE

Since 1967 the Conference Board has been collecting data for a monthly Consumer Confidence Index (CCI) using surveys with 5,000 representative U.S. households. The surveys focus on five basic questions:

1. How do you see current business conditions?
2. How do you foresee business conditions in the next six months?
3. What's your view of employment conditions?
4. What do you think of employment conditions for the next six months?
5. What's your prediction for total family income over the next six months?[173]

The year 1985 is taken as "baseline" year and has been assigned a value of 100. Therefore, one could interpret each monthly reading as a comparison to the general confidence level in 1985. Readings well below 100 would signal that consumers are much less confident than they were in 1985, while the opposite is the case for readings above 100. The CCI is used by producers, among others, as a way to help predict likely consumer demand. But because it is a measure of opinion, the CCI indicates how people feel about their present situation and their outlook for the future. During an Arrogance Cycle, there may be plenty of confidence— but how much of it is based on rosy optimism rather than real productivity?

Consumer Confidence is reported monthly by the Conference Board. For our analysis, we used the trailing three-month average reading to arrive at a quarter figure for Consumer Confidence. The highs and lows in the CCI between March of 1990 and June of 2010 have been dramatic.

Obviously, the outlook of consumers becomes sharply more pessimistic following notable market declines. In the early 1990s, with people feeling negative about the economy, the CCI was in the 50 to 70 percent range, with people feeling negative about their current situations and their futures. But then along comes the dot-com boom, and by 1998 the CCI is on a steep climb that reaches 140 in the year 2000. Similarly, when the market bottoms out in 2008, consumer confidence sinks by 100 points.

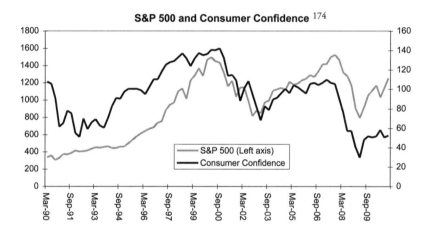

S&P 500 and Consumer Confidence [174]

TYING IT ALL TOGETHER

In the chart on the next page, we show how closely our regression tracks the S&P 500. It should be noticed that these three variables have historically been able to produce a relatively accurate level for the S&P 500. Therefore, if you can make assumptions with regard to these three variables, you can produce a very rough level for where the S&P 500 should be trading.[175]

WHAT'S IT ALL MEAN?

As noted, our Arrogance Index provides some very interesting insight into market behavior. Since it's not a surefire predictor

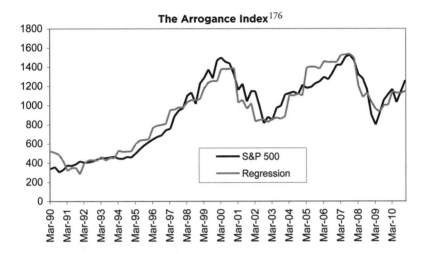

The Arrogance Index[176]

of trends, I wouldn't make any serious investment commitment based on the Arrogance Index alone. But as an indicator of where the market is going, it provides a very provocative assessment. When all three indicators are telling us an Arrogance Cycle is on the upswing, investors would be wise to be on the lookout for a bubble—with all the danger this implies.

While these visible signs of a rising Arrogance Cycle are detectable using the metrics I have just described, we have also seen that there are less easily measured indicators just below the surface. Taken as a whole, one might describe these other forces as the sucking sounds of arrogance. Inevitably, the aggregation of these forces will pop the bubble. Whether it happens sooner or later is anyone's guess, but as sure as night follows day, these subsurface factors are certain to implode when the bubble explodes.

- *Swindles are bound to rise.*

With so many investors caught in the updraft of rising aspirations, inevitably there will be hucksters, shysters, and other "–sters" to take advantage of the feeding frenzy. As paragons of sleaze have so clearly demonstrated in recent decades, a mastery of technology combined with basic obfuscation techniques can produce a startling amount of deception. Just below the surface of a bubble, schemes are sure to proliferate, if only because there is so much money looking for places to go. Of course, a silver tongue and the right connections also help the process along. But the bubbly atmosphere is what really gives swindlers the upper hand. Everyone's eagerness to slide out from under the bell of the bell curve—to prove themselves far above average—makes for a lot of willing targets for those who are in the business of nurturing illusions, twisting arms, and fudging reports.

- *Fear feeds unbalanced behavior.*

Also increasing as the bubble rises is the element of fear, doing its eternal pas de deux with greed. Of course, it's an emotion that the arrogant don't like to admit to—and, like any emotion that must be hidden, denial only adds to its secret power. What's extraordinary is the way fear cripples the ability to think or react rationally.

For example, an investor can be fully aware that stocks are overpriced, yet, driven by fear of failure, that investor will plunge ahead wildly as if—*This time! For the first time in history!*—the bubble were sustainable. He knows it isn't, but he goes there anyway; then, he's too far in and lives in fear that it will all collapse. As the market bravely marches into territory where it has never gone before, as promises like "It will be different this time" begin to whisper sweet nothings in our ears, one has only to look at the chart of past market behavior to feel the fear. We know that what rises must fall. How far? How fast? When? Those are the only real questions.

Fear that the inevitable *will* happen puts the arrogant investor in a dangerous position of denial. One side of his brain is saying, "It can't and it won't," while the other side declares "It shall and it must." Caught in the middle, he puts up a bold front, even as his hands are trembling.

- *There is more show than tell.*

A gleaming bubble is shiny with promise, but the larger it grows, the emptier it seems. Can we keep pretending that what we see is what we get? This is a question that becomes increasingly difficult to answer as the bubble rises. It's unsettling for the cautious and conscientious investor who wants to look at the fundamentals before he commits. There's so much window dressing. "What *looks* good *must* be good," becomes the mantra. As the underlying fundamentals are perceived to be less important, more people are sold the sizzle. If few are concerned with real value, if a stock is soaring based on perception alone, it stands to reason the people backing that stock (managers of the company, for instance) are going to work very hard on improving the *perception* of value. The car gets a bright new paint job, and the salespeople go to work selling it, hoping no one will ask whether the engine is running or not.

THE AFTERMATH OF ARROGANCE

Of course, the really annoying thing about any Arrogance Cycle is that some people do get very rich in the bubble, and some manage to stay that way even when it bursts. Those in the pilot seat who manage to keep their calm may have the consolation of a smooth landing and may feel the satisfaction of having weathered the storm. But there's also the possibility that the reckless, arrogant guys who thrived on the bubble did some real damage to our purses, our economy, and—I hate to say it—our nation.

In the plunge of '08, brought on by the most severe Arrogance Cycle in recent history, we saw the savings and investments of far too many hardworking middle-class Americans utterly gutted by the stock market and housing collapses. Unemployment soared as gas escaped the bubble and it burst into a thousand fragments. Retirees found their nest eggs decimated. Kids saw their moms and dads clawing at meager hope while banks and collection agencies bombarded their homes with messages, telling them to pay up or get out. Photographs of FORECLOSED signs on front lawns and emptied-out shelves in food kitchens became iconic images of a recession that we shall no doubt always recall with a shudder of dread. To some of the 1 percent who earn 20 percent of the income, the whole ghastly game with CDOs and credit default swaps may have been an amusing pastime, but to those who felt the exhaust of arrogance choking their lungs, it was one hell of a nasty experience.

No question: To many of us, the ultra-arrogant are the enemy. The trouble is, there's a human tendency to believe that the best way to get back at your enemy is by behaving like them. And while that might work on the battlefield, it generally doesn't work with investments. We don't gain any advantage by becoming more arrogant, and there's a good chance that, in so doing, we will only put ourselves at greater risk than before.

NEW TOOLS FOR BETTER DECISION-MAKING

In the previous chapter, I gave you a quick Arrogance Scale survey to gain some insight into your arrogance level. In this chapter, I've described the objective measurements that will tell you when the Arrogance Cycle is headed toward a new high. Combining these two tools will, I hope, give you a degree of objectivity that could be very helpful in your decision-making process. If your personal Arrogance Cycle is on an upswing, you'll be more confident that you can "read" the market—that you know what's going to happen, that you can follow your gut feelings, and that you'll come out ahead of the average guy. All these are sure signs of arrogance. Combine a high-number egotype with arrogance factors in the market—a soaring Consumer Confidence Index, increased income concentrated in a small proportion of the population, a neglect of personal savings—and you can see that it's time to put on the brakes. Rising inner arrogance and a soaring Arrogance

Cycle should produce warning signals that flash before your eyes. I would advise you to grab a 'chute that is made of the toughest cloth available and float your way to a safe landing. You may miss out on playing with the big guys. You might even miss a jackpot or two. But believe me, it's a lot easier to land in one piece when the controls are still on.

But wait; who's telling you this? A conservative kind of guy? You bet. Someone who believes you can participate in financial markets without being the cagiest guy in town? An investor who has made some whopping big mistakes, has seen the market do some really unpredictable things, and still thinks trading on the future of the United States is a very good way to do business? Yes, that's me.

I do believe it's possible to keep arrogance in check and to factor in the cycles without succumbing to them. Do the homework that needs to be done. Keep the rulebook open, identify the slick guys who aren't playing by it, and stay with the solid guys who are.

I also believe runaway arrogance can get us in big trouble. I mean major, major, major trouble—to the point where one bunch of sweaty bankers pulling a few all-nighters are in a position to decide whether the world's economy will collapse or keep running. I've seen runaway arrogance reach that level just once in my lifetime, and that's enough, thank you. If it never happens again, that will be too soon for me.

I don't know about you, but there was one day in 2008 when my wife and I looked at each other, drove to the bank, pulled out some standby cash, brought it home, and put it in the safest place we could find. You know . . . just in case. And I'm not the kind of guy who panics.

Do I ever want to do that again?

Not in my lifetime, I hope. And not in my kids' lifetimes either.

CHAPTER 9

YOUR HUMILITY INDEX

"Remember Thou Art Mortal"

A president during his impeachment hearing, Wall Street CEOs as they do the handcuffed perp walk, and I myself, before my *complete*, annual physical, are three examples of evident humility. Can you think about your humble moments? Go ahead; it's kind of fun in a sick way. When the cop asks for your license and registration, in the moment before you receive an exam score, when your tee shot fells some grandmother in the gallery, or when your cell-phone records become public (and your wife attacks you with a seven-iron) may be moments that make your list. Can you hear the collective groan and feel that awful feeling? Your behavior changes, too, doesn't it? Some become quiet and speak in hushed tones while others chatter mindlessly. But whatever your response, you do behave differently.

Humble moments are not bet-the-farm, go-for-it moments. Humble moments are for reflection, protection, and self-preservation. If the greatest financial deal of your entire life was presented to you at a humble moment, would you be able to seize it? Could you act? Or would you miss it in your moment of paralysis?

Humility is one of those words like *average*—perfectly fine as long as it's being applied to someone else. Webster's defines humble as *not proud or haughty; not arrogant or assertive.* I think of the milquetoast characters like Uncle Billy in *It's a Wonderful Life*. Periods of humility strike me as laudable for the truly accomplished.

I just struggle to imagine having much of a cocktail party with a herd of the humble.

Talk of humility tends to be bandied about in religious circles, but when the religious leaders who are bandying it about turn arrogant, it definitely loses some of its oomph. It also gets confused with its near cousin, humiliation, and certainly no one likes to be humiliated.

So I may be setting myself a tough job, but in this chapter I'd like to try to restore some of the luster to what was once thought to be a very admirable quality of character. And while I don't know whether I'll succeed in convincing you, I would, at the very least, like to give you some respect for humility as a countervailing force to be applied against arrogance—your own and others'.

The fact is, anyone who has spent any amount of time in the investment world has been forced to eat humble pie. We fell in love with a company that was undeserving of our adoration or attention. We perceived a market aberration as the sign of a new trend, only to discover (too late!) that it was a deceptive blip. We did the math based on our knowledge of one sector but neglected to pay attention to an element of chaos in some other part of the economy that ultimately KO'd our strategy. We take it on the chin, hope to keep learning, and try to find a few sweet raisins in the stale old humble pie that's mostly hard crust.

What happens if you raise your humility index? Not only does it help counterbalance arrogance, but some humility can also be extremely helpful when you're winding your way through the decision-making process. The really cool part about humility is that it's quiet, and it knows how to listen. It is the antipode of arrogance. Humility questions, confers, and reflects. It is patient and deliberate. Humility itself is actually a very good tool to have in your investment portfolio. Here are ten ways to make humility work for you when you're designing an investment strategy.

1. *Accept Your Limits*

You don't know everything, and you can't know everything. You may gather information, study, and analyze, but in the end you have to make a judgment call. Your research will help mitigate but not eliminate risk. After years of experience, lots of research, and applying a rational discipline, you *will* still be wrong sometimes. And you will be right sometimes. (I didn't emphasize the "will" in that second sentence, because we need to maintain humility about being right.)

Remember that being great at one thing doesn't make you great at everything. While one skill set may help you with other challenges and tasks, it is important to be vigilant against the type of presumptuous transference that results in arrogance.

After the tech wreck of 2001, lots of new clients showed up on the doorsteps of lots of money managers with the same tale. *I need your help. I was doing just fine with my portfolio through the nineties, but now I'm losing my ass. I used to get this stuff, but now it's killing me. I need a professional to do this for me. Anything will be better than what I'm doing.* Another Arrogance Cycle had come and gone, and their egomaniacal certainty was now a thing of the past. People who were comfortable taking responsibility for gains can't endure the consequence of losing. The ironic part is that given their experience of loss and their walk through the dark valley of unsuccessful risks taken, they are better prepared to shepherd their own investments than they were when they were enjoying success.

2. *Sacrifice Certainty*

Bubbles do begin with a plausible, fundamental argument, or "truth." What's difficult is acknowledging that one truth (in the market) doesn't last forever. Malthus proved the folly of slavishly following a theory that's based on the assumption that one trend will continue forever. We are surrounded by an ever-changing landscape, so we always need to remember that yesterday's valid thesis may be invalidated tomorrow by today's new developments. Bubble builders often cling desperately to their truth even when they're confronted with clear evidence of opposing facts. It's okay to be uncertain. Give doubt some room to grow. Well-considered doubts may be more reliable than accepted truths that have seen their day.

3. *Acknowledge Your Need to Belong*

The standard nag from our generation's mothers was, "Well, if all of your friends jumped off a bridge, would you jump, too?" This was the antidote to arguments like: "Come on, Mom. All the other kids are going." "Cary's mom says it's fine with her." "It will be totally safe; there will be upperclassmen to supervise."

Do you remember things that you hadn't tried but were convinced you had to? Weren't you sure that, whatever this novelty may have been, it was going to be the greatest thing in your life? There is a reason that I'm citing adolescent memories. Adolescence is an action-packed time that could benefit from a little more thought.

Over time, a herd mentality will turn plausibility into certainty. (That's particularly the case when there are rising profits.) Trends often last longer than anyone expects, and as you see more and more people following a trend, no doubt you're going to begin to feel very left out. It's an uneasy feeling. Not pleasant. But that feeling shouldn't force you to feel you have to join the herd. Acknowledge it, review your position, make the choices that are right for you, and move on.

Picture stampeding herds moving at top speed, surrounded by clouds of dust. The trampled aftermath isn't good for grazing or much of anything else. In Dante's *Divine Comedy,* those souls damned to the realm of the lustful are described as being blown about on the unpredictable gusts of passion like flocks of starlings that rise, fall, turn, and return without thought or purpose. Can you feel yourself being blown about by the gusts of greed and the fear of missing out, leaving your reasonable, questioning, rational self at the door?

4. *Recognize Your Envy*

Envy is one of the seven deadly sins. Frederick Buechner defines *envy* as the consuming desire to have everybody else be as unsuccessful as you are. Buechner captures the meanness of envy, but not the aching desire for other people's stuff, or how bad their having it accentuates the painful reality that you don't.

If you're not in the hot sector of the market, you may feel like you've missed out. And maybe you have! Maybe there are a bunch of folks who got in ahead of you and made a killing. There's no reason *not* to be jealous; go ahead. Just don't let envy dictate your next move. If you do, you'll be following the herd rather than thinking for yourself. Don't try to find fresh grass where everyone else has grazed.

We have a rule at our firm: We will always sacrifice opportunity rather than sacrifice clients' capital. When it comes to envy, make sure you don't sacrifice your principles either. Machiavelli was pretty savvy about politics but didn't have the keys to investment advice.

5. *Remember—You're* Not *the Brightest Bulb!*

Do you sense a new trend on the horizon? Do you see something about to happen that others are blind to? Careful; you may be momentarily awed by your personal insight, understanding, or vision—but it's unlikely you're the only genius spotting an opportunity. If others are failing to "see the obvious" and pluck the golden apple, there may be a reason.

My sixty-six-year-old investor from Florida—the one who got into real estate—learned this lesson in a devastatingly expensive way. There are always downsides.

It's never easy to miss out on an opportunity—and really *good* missed opportunities are harder yet to live with. But even if you "miss out" on making a lot of money, the decision that you make could still be the right one *for you*. Profit can't be the only validation.

About the same time that my Florida guy was investing in houses, a young man named Jeff Barnette asked to meet with me to discuss a fund he wanted my help starting. He explained that buying credit default swaps on CDOs was a license to steal. Michael Lewis in his fabulous book, *The Big Short*, explained the hundreds of billions of dollars that were made using this theory. When this brilliant young man explained to me how much money could be made, I turned him down. Nothing could be that easy, I thought. I had to be missing something, but I was much too experienced and wise to be wooed by that siren song.

Turns out that a $100,000 investment would have wrought something over $15 million in fewer than two years. Was it painful to realize that I'd missed my chance there? Indeed. It's very hard to say that I made a good decision. It cost me millions of dollars, but it was *still* a good decision.

6. *In a Typhoon, Batten Down the Hatches*

Often, your "mediocre" but safer holdings will weather the storm of the bubbles bursting better than anything else. Be a great student. Do your homework. Find out what you want to hold on to. Know what you own, and understand how the company makes money. Make decisions with your head and not with your gut or your heart. Then stay firm when the storm hits.

When skies are clear and breezes are light, even the most inexperienced seaman can take the helm, but when winds howl and the sea churns, we all want the most seasoned captain at the helm.

7. *Show Some Respect for History*

Those who say of trends in the market, "It's different this time," will ultimately realize that it's not different this time. The markets always return to the mean. Again, remember Malthus, the first great and wrong economist.

Investing requires a mind that is open to change and emerging possibilities. What will a cure for cancer mean not just to the human condition but to economic productivity and share prices? Remember the world before the Internet? When I started Farr, Miller & Washington in 1996, we bragged that we had computers on every desk and were investigating a new technology that would allow our telephones to dial into a fairly new service called America Online.

Imagine how the world would change if tomorrow some long-haired, dope-smoking genius showed up on *The Today Show* with just-add-water wafers that were made from sand that you could put into your car's gas tank or your furnace to provide all the energy you could need for less than $10 a year! Just when you think you've got the world figured out, count on some pothead to do something fabulous that may change the world.

8. *Fold 'Em When You Have To*

In the sitcom *Happy Days* that originally aired from 1974 to 1984, Henry Winkler played a super-cool biker, mechanic, and chick magnet who could not say the word "wrong." He would open his mouth and begin with "wrrrrrr . . . wrrrrrrrrrooooo . . . wrrrrrrrrrrrrrr-roooooooo . . . ," and then simply declare that he couldn't do it. Not all of your investments will bear fruit. Professionals are usually thrilled if 60 percent of their decisions work out. Knowing when to cut your losses is critical. Riding a mistake to zero because you're too proud to sell it is a steep price to pay for arrogance. Accept that you may need to get out of a certain sector of the market sooner rather than later, without getting every last scrap from the table.

Wall Street's saying is, "Bulls and Bears make money while Pigs get slaughtered." It may feel bad to sell at a loss, but sometimes you just have to do what feels bad. Look to the future. Knowing when to push away from the table may save your chips.

9. *Embrace the Fear*

As Warren Buffett noted, "We try to be greedy when others are fearful and fearful when others are greedy." The fear in others may be preventing them from doing what should be done. Conversely, when you feel your own fear—brought on by risking too much or too often—don't turn away. Your fear is trying to tell you something. Better listen.

Arrogant investors aren't fearful. They won't tolerate fear or even the discussion of why they *might* be afraid. If you can honestly acknowledge that you might be completely wrong at the genesis of every investment, you'll be making better, safer decisions.

10. *Do It for Someone Else*

I have the privilege of serving on the board of trustees of Sibley Memorial Hospital in Washington, D.C. As you might expect, I am on almost every financial committee they have, including the investment committee. As our committee deliberates over decisions about deploying the hospital's assets, we are very much aware of our roles as stewards of a community asset. Stewardship is sobering. Stewardship is defined by Webster's as *the careful and responsible management of something entrusted to one's care.*

Often you make better decisions if they're not all about you. What's best for your family? If you make money, what can you give away, and where? If you're taking big risks, is it for the sake of buying toys or improving your quality of life? If you're getting a generous amount of what you deserve, can you also deserve to be generous? You might find you make your best decisions when you're working for the benefit of someone else.

Before taking the plunge, ask yourself if you'd continue to buy if you were responsible for the stewardship of these funds.

◆

The Arrogance Cycle is always at hand. We are always at some point on our own arrogance continuum. Quivering insecurity and fear, or the bulletproof, superhuman sense of infallible certainty—both can overwhelm judgment and reason. Healthy, deliberate decisions naturally drive better results. If you're not sure how you're feeling, go to www.arrogancecycle.com and take our online self-test.

You will always hear and see the clanging bells and flashing lights from the million-dollar slot-machine winners and wonder, "What if that had been my quarter?" *But*, if you find yourself believing that the very quarter in your hand will absolutely, without a doubt, be the coin that liberates the million-dollar jackpot, it may be time to conduct a checkup from the neck up and determine your arrogance score.

Julius Caesar had a slave assigned to follow him through adoring crowds, whispering, "Remember thou art mortal."

I am delighted to celebrate all readers: May you surpass all of your goals and dreams, achieve every success in your investing future and, above all, never forget the lessons learned from Arrogance Cycles.

ACKNOWLEDGMENTS

I am very grateful to so many friends and colleagues who helped with this book. Ed Claflin, in addition to being a very bright, talented, good guy, was an outstanding collaborator. It has been a pleasure and honor working with Ed.

Once again, Scott Sobel pushed me to write another book. Keith B. Davis, CFA, helped me construct the Arrogance Index, and worked tirelessly and brilliantly to make me look good. Keith's name should be on the cover.

My great friend, P. J. O'Rourke, is a constant support and mentor for all of my literary activities. P. J. has written a great foreword, and I am exceptionally honored and grateful.

Psychiatrists Harvey Rich, MD, and Curtis Bristol, MD, were hugely helpful with their time, intellect, and insight.

Thank you to all of my friends at CNBC for your encouragement.

My agents Jane Dystel and Miriam Goderich have been amazing. They helped me sort through offers and led me to Globe Pequot and the great Janice Goldklang. Janice has embraced this book from the beginning, edited with enthusiasm, caring, and a judicious eye. Many thanks to everyone at Globe Pequot Press.

Jonathan Duber from Cornell University was a fabulous research analyst and strategist.

My sincere thanks to great friends Sally Cutler and Jack Biddle for their proofreading and weighing in with their candid insights and thoughtful comments.

Thank you to Frank, Michael, Bob, Cary, Fred, Roy, Steve, Jimmy, Corky, and all of the Gillionville Brainstormers.

Thank you to those brave souls who suffered my presence in their classrooms: Ray Lelii, S.J., Rick Cannon, John Reishman,

Dale Richardson, Tam Carlson, Bill Clarkson, Bob Benson, Tim Keith-Lucas, Rene Soudee, Tom Dixon, and Bob Wipfler.

Finally, thank you to everyone at Farr, Miller & Washington: Susan Cantus, Sunny Miller, John Washington, Taylor McGowan, Caroline Savage, Keith Davis, Chris Meeker, Michael Fox, Glenn Ryhanych, Darshan Gulati, George Williams, Steven Stone, Javier Madariaga, Grace Santos, Sheldon Cohen, Jenifer Gregory, Chris White, and Joe Coreth.

NOTES

1   "The State of Consumption Today," Worldwatch Institute, www
    .worldwatch.org/node/810.
2   "Credit Card Statistics, Industry Facts, Debt Statistics," Credit
    Cards.com, www.creditcards.com/credit-card-news/credit-card-
    industry-facts-personal-debt-statistics-1276.php.
3   Frederick Lewis Allen, *Only Yesterday: An Informal History of the
    1920s* (Harper, 2000), 276.
4   http://www.census.gov/hhes/www/housing/census/historic/owner
    .html.
5   "Comparison of the U.S. to Other Rich Nations," The Reagan
    Years: A Statistical Overview of the 1980s, www.huppi.com/
    kangaroo/8Comparison.htm.
6   William D. Cohan, *House of Cards: A Tale of Hubris and Wretched
    Excess on Wall Street* (Doubleday, 2009), Kindle ed., loc. 5954–59.
7   All quotes from "Francisco's Money Speech," Ayn Rand, *Atlas
    Shrugged,* quoted on www.capitalismmagazine.com/economics/
    money/1826-francisco-s-money-speech.html.
8   Jason Zweig, *Your Money and Your Brain: How the New Science
    of Neuroeconomics Can Help Make You Rich* (Simon & Schuster,
    2007), Kindle ed., loc. 1180–84.
9   Zweig, loc. 1210–15.
10 Lori F. Cummins, Michael R. Nadorff, Anita E. Kelly, "Winning
    and Positive Affect Can Lead to Reckless Gambling," *Psychology of
    Addictive Behaviors*, Vol. 23, No. 2 (June 2009), 287–94.
11 Ibid., 289.
12 M. J. Rockloff and V. Dyer, "An Experiment on the Social Facilita-
    tion of Gambling Behavior," *Journal of Gambling Studies*, March
    2007.
13 http://usgovinfo.about.com/library/weekly/aa060401a.htm.

14 "Median and Average Sales Prices of New Homes Sold in United States," U.S. Census Bureau, www.census.gov/const/uspriceann .pdf.

15 "Mortgage Rate—30-Year (Recent History), Data360, www.data 360.org/dsg.aspx?Data_Set_Group_Id=245&page=4&count=100.

16 "The 401(k) Turns 20," CNNMoney, http://money.cnn .com/2001/01/04/strategies/q_retire_401k/index.htm.

17 "A Brief History of the 401(k)," *Time,* www.time.com/time/ magazine/article/0,9171,1851124,00.html.

18 Frank J. Fabozzi and Franco Modigliani, *Mortgage and Mortgage-Backed Securities Markets* (Harvard Business School Press, 1992), 31.

19 Gillian Tett, *Fool's Gold: How the Bold Dream of a Small Tribe at J.P. Morgan was Corrupted by Wall Street Greed and Unleashed Catastrophe* (Simon & Schuster, 2009), Kindle ed.

20 Tett, loc. 112–17.

21 Tett, loc. 19.

22 Tett, loc. 248–53.

23 Tett, loc. 149–55 and 155–60.

24 Tett, loc. 1223–28.

25 Tett, loc. 1346.

26 Ibid.

27 Tett, loc. 3539.

28 "Buffett Warns on Investment Time Bomb," BBC News, http:// news.bbc.co.uk/2/hi/2817995.stm.

29 Lawrence G. McDonald with Patrick Robinson, *A Colossal Failure of Common Sense: The Inside Story of the Collapse of Lehman Brothers,* (Crown Business, 2009), Kindle ed., loc. 6135.

30 McDonald, loc. 6314.

31 McDonald, loc. 6325.

32 McDonald, loc. 6406.

33 McDonald, loc. 6491.

34 McDonald, loc. 6492.

35 McDonald, loc. 2133.

36 McDonald, loc. 1702.

37 McDonald, loc. 2501.

38 McDonald, loc. 1811.

39 McDonald, loc. 1834.

40 McDonald, loc. 1830.

41 McDonald, loc. 6428.

42 McDonald, loc. 6546.

43 Kara Scannell and Sudeep Reddy, "Greenspan Admits Errors to Hostile House Panel," *The Wall Street Journal,* October 24, 2008, http://online.wsj.com/article/SB122476545437862295.html.

44 "Greenspeak," Federal Reserve Bank of Dallas, www.dallasfed.org/news/speeches/greenspeak.html.

45 Ibid.

46 Ibid.

47 Nell Henderson, "Bernanke: There's No Housing Bubble to Go Bust," *The Washington Post,* October 27, 2005, www.washingtonpost.com/wp-dyn/content/article/2005/10/26/AR2005102602255.html.

48 "Remarks by Vice Chairman Roger W. Ferguson Jr.," The Federal Reserve Board, www.federalreserve.gov/boarddocs/speeches/2005/20051128/default.htm.

49 Scannell, "Greenspan Admits Errors."

50 "Goldman Sachs Trader 'Fabulous' Fabrice Tourre's Conflicted Love Letters," *New York Daily News,* April 26, 2010, www.nydailynews.com/money/2010/04/26/2010-04-26_goldman_sachs_trader_fabulous_fabrice_tourres_conflicted_love_letters.html?page=1.

51 Ben White, "What Red Ink? Wall Street Paid Hefty Bonuses," *The New York Times,* January 28, 2009, www.nytimes.com/2009/01/29/business/29bonus.html.

52 Harry Markopolos, *No One Would Listen: A True Financial Thriller* (Wiley, 2010), Kindle edition, loc. 688.

53 Markopolos, loc. 662.

54 Markopolos, loc. 679.

55 Markopolos, loc. 588.

56 Markopolos, loc. 609.

57 Markopolos, loc. 615.

58 Markopolos, loc. 736.

59 Markopolos, loc. 788.

60 Markopolos, loc. 911.

61 Ibid.

62 Markopolos, loc. 3973.

63 Steve Fishman, "Bernie Madoff, Free at Last," *New York Magazine*, June 6, 2010, http://nymag.com/news/crimelaw/66468/.

64 The repeal of this act was signed by Clinton on November 12, 1999.

65 Cohan, *House of Cards*, loc. 8278–84; $525 billion assets on $12 billion of equity.

66 Cohan, loc. 2554.

67 Cohan, loc. 2406–11.

68 Jesse Kornbluth, *Highly Confident: The Crime and Punishment of Michael Milken* (William Morrow and Company, 1992).

69 Dan G. Stone, *April Fools: An Insider's Account of the Rise and Collapse of Drexel Burnham* (Donald I. Fine, 1990).

70 "Drexel Sues Milken, Seeking Repayment," *The New York Times*, September 12, 1991; "Milken to Pay $500 Million More in $1.3 Billion Drexel Settlement," *The New York Times*, February 18, 1992.

71 Kurt Eichenwald, *Conspiracy of Fools: A True Story* (Broadway, 2005), Kindle edition, loc. 6404–10.

72 Eichenwald, loc. 6410–16.

73 Eichenwald, loc. 6416–21.

74 Eichenwald, loc. 6410–16.

75 Bill Saporito, "How Fastow Helped Enron Fall," *Time*, www.time.com/time/business/article/0,8599,201871,00.html.

76 Ibid.

77 Eichenwald, loc. 4139.

78 Dennis Moberg and Edward Romar, "WorldCom," Markkula Center for Applied Ethics, Santa Clara University, www.scu.edu/ethics/dialogue/candc/cases/worldcom.html.

79 E. S. Browning, "Is the Praise for WorldCom Too Much?" *The Wall Street Journal,* October 8, 1997, C-24. All acquisition amounts are taken from this article. Quoted in Moberg et al.

80 G. Colvin, "Wonder Women of Whistleblowing," *Fortune,* August 12, 2002, 56+; S. Pelliam and D. Solomon, "Uncooking the Books: How Three Unlikely Sleuths Discovered Fraud at World-Com," *The Wall Street Journal,* October 30, 2002, A-1.

81 Mark Pittman, "Goldman, Merrill Collect Billions after Fed's AIG Bailout Loans," Bloomberg News, September 29, 2008.

82 Gretchen Morgenson, "Behind Insurer's Crisis, Blind Eye to a Web of Risk," *The New York Times,* September 27, 2008.

83 Ibid.

84 U.S. Federal Reserve Board of Governors, Press Release: "Federal Reserve Board, Met with Full Support of the Treasury Department, Authorizes the Federal Reserve Bank of New York to Lend up to $85 billion to the American International Group (AIG), September 16, 2008."

85 "Testimony of Joseph J. Cassano Before the Financial Crisis Inquiry Commission, June 30, 2010, http://c0182412.cdn1.cloudfiles.rackspacecloud.com/2010-0630-Cassano.pdf www.fcic.gov/hearings/pdfs/2010-0630-Cassano.pdf.

86 Gary Gorton, "The Panic of 2007," Yale School of Management and NBER, www.som.yale.edu/faculty/gbg24/Panic%20of%202007.pdf.

87 Ibid.

88 Karen Gullo, "Former AIG Executive Cassano Said Not to Face Charges in Insurer's Failure," Bloomberg, www.bloomberg.com/news/2010-05-22/u-s-prosecutors-said-to-drop-probe-of-former-aig-executive-joseph-cassano.html.

89   Edward Chancellor, *Devil Take the Hindmost: A History of Financial Speculation* (Penguin/Plume, 1999), 14.
90   Chancellor, 19.
91   Chancellor, 25.
92   Chancellor, 17.
93   Chancellor, 19.
94   Chancellor, 51.
95   Chancellor, 101.
96   Chancellor, 128.
97   Chancellor, 177.
98   Chancellor, 63.
99   Chancellor, 66.
100   Chancellor, 63.
101   Chancellor, 64.
102   Chancellor, 65.
103   Chancellor, 73.
104   Chancellor, 70.
105   Chancellor, 72.
106   Chancellor, 83.
107   Allen, 290.
108   Allen, 290.
109   Allen, 259.
110   Allen, 260.
111   Allen, 253.
112   Allen, 267.
113   Ibid.
114   John Kenneth Galbraith, *The Great Crash 1929* (Mariner Books, 1997), 108.
115   Chancellor, 192.
116   Ibid.
117   Allen, 141.
118   Allen, 142.
119   Allen, 143.

120 Chancellor, 197.

121 Chancellor, 199.

122 Allen, 251.

123 Chancellor, 198.

124 Chancellor, 209.

125 Chancellor, 201.

126 Ibid.

127 John Maynard Keynes, *The General Theory of Employment, Interest and Money* (1936), quoted in Chancellor, 222.

128 Trading statistics for the 1920s from *Only Yesterday,* 264. Statistics for 2010 from http://www.money-zine.com/Investing/Stocks/New-York-Stock-Exchange/.

129 "Gramm-Leach-Bliley Act," Wikipedia, http://en.wikipedia.org/wiki/Gramm%E2%80%93Leach%E2%80%93Bliley_Act.

130 This, and the following information, comes from two sources: "Carter Glass and the Federal Reserve Act of 1913," Suburban Emergency Management Project, www.semp.us/publications/biot_printview.php?BiotID=605; and "Carter Glass," Wikipedia, http://en.wikipedia.org/wiki/Carter_Glass.

131 Note: Wilson, like Glass, was preoccupied with the close relationship between banks and their customers. In a commentary that seems as applicable today as it was in 1912, Wilson wrote: "You will notice from a recent investigation that things like this take place: A certain bank invests in certain securities. It appears from evidence that the handling of these securities was very intimately connected with the maintenance of the price of a particular commodity. Nobody ought, and in normal circumstances nobody would, for a moment think of suspecting the managers of a great bank of making such an investment in order to help those who were conducting a particular business in the United States to maintain the price of their commodity; but the circumstances are not normal. It is beginning to be believed that in the big business of this

country nothing is disconnected from anything else. I do not mean in this particular instance to which I referred, and I do not have in mind to draw any inference at all, for that would be unjust; but take any investment of an industrial character by a great bank. It is known that the directorate of that bank interlaces in personnel with ten, twenty, thirty, forty, fifty, sixty boards of directors of all sorts, of railroads which handle commodities, of great groups of manufacturers which manufacture commodities, and of great merchants who distribute commodities; and the result is that every great bank is under suspicion with regard to the motive of its investment. It is at least considered possible that it is playing the game of somebody who has nothing to do with banking, but with whom some of its directors are connected and joined in interest. The ground of unrest and uneasiness, in short, on the part of the public at large, is the growing knowledge that many large undertakings are interlaced with one another, indistinguishable from one another in personnel.

"Therefore, when a small group of men approach Congress in order to induce the committee concerned to concur in certain legislation, nobody knows the ramifications of the interest which those men represent; there seems no frank and open action of public opinion in public counsel, but every man is suspected of representing some other man, and it is not known where his connections begin or end." (Woodrow Wilson: *The New Freedom, A Call for the Emancipation of the Generous Energies of a People*. Original copyright, New York, 1913. Republished by BibioBazaar 2007, the Kessinger Pub, 2008).

132   "Carter Glass and the Federal Reserve Act of 1913."

133   Rixey Smith and Norman Beasley, *Carter Glass: A Biography* (Longmans, Green and Co., 1939), 286–87.

134   "Carter Glass and the Federal Reserve Act of 1913."

135   Smith and Beasley, 296–98.

136 "The Long Demise of Glass-Steagall," *Frontline,* PBS.org, www
.pbs.org/wgbh/pages/frontline/shows/wallstreet/weill/demise
.html.

137 Ibid.

138 Michael Quint, "Federal Reserve Acts to Let Banks into Bond
Trading," *The New York Times*, January 19, 1989.

139 "Carter Glass and the Federal Reserve Act of 1913."

140 Ibid.

141 Barbara Ley Toffler, *Final Accounting: Ambition, Greed and the
Fall of Arthur Andersen* (Broadway Books, 2003), loc. 822ff.

142 "History of the SEC," *Bill Moyers Journal,* www.pbs.org/moyers/
journal/10122007/sec.html.

143 "U.S. Securities and Exchange Commission," Wikipedia, http://
en.wikipedia.org/wiki/U.S._Securities_and_Exchange
_Commission.

144 "What Is the Number of Publicly Traded Companies in the
U.S.?," Answers.com, http://wiki.answers.com/Q/What_is_the_
number_of_publicly_traded_companies_in_the_US.

145 "U.S. Securities and Exchange Commission," U.S. Economy, About.com, http://useconomy.about.com/od/
governmentagencies/p/SEC.htm.

146 "SEC's Cox: 'Gravely Concerned' About 'Multiple Failures' in
Madoff Case," Washington Wire (WSJ Blogs), *The Wall Street
Journal,* http://blogs.wsj.com/washwire/2008/12/16/secs-cox-
gravely-concerned-about-multiple-failures-in-madoff-case/.

147 Zachery Kouwe, "In Harsh Reports on S.E.C.'s Fraud Failures, a
Watchdog Urges Sweeping Changes," *The New York Times,* September 29, 2009, www.nytimes.com/2009/09/30/business/30sec
.html?_r=2.

148 Ibid.

149 Cecilia Kang, "Report Says SEC Failed in Oversight of Bear
Stearns," *The Washington Post,* September 27, 2008, www
.washingtonpost.com/wp-dyn/content/article/2008/09/26/
AR2008092603489.html?hpid=topnews.

150 "Christopher Cox," Wikipedia, http://en.wikipedia.org/wiki/ Christopher_Cox.

151 SEC Press Release: "Chairman Cox Announces End of Consolidated Supervised Entities Program," September 26, 2008, www .sec.gov/news/press/2008/2008-230.htm.

152 Alex Wagner, "Obama Signs Financial Reform Bill, Hails New Safeguards," Politics Daily, www.politicsdaily.com/2010/07/21/ obama-signs-financial-reform-bill-all-smiles-with-pelosi-and-re/.

153 "Household Debt Service and Financial Obligations Ratios," The Federal Reserve Board, www.federalreserve.gov/releases/ housedebt/.

154 "National Economic Accounts," Bureau of Economic Analysis, www.bea.gov/briefrm/saving.htm.

155 G. William Domhoff, "Wealth, Income, and Power," *Who Rules America?*, Sociology Department, University of California at Santa Cruz, http://sociology.ucsc.edu/whorulesamerica/power/ wealth.html.

156 "Advertising and Branding Industry Overview," Plunkett Research, Ltd., www.plunkettresearch.com/Industries/ AdvertisingandBranding/AdvertisingandBrandingStatistics/ tabid/70/Default.aspx.

157 "Thomas Robert Malthus," Wikipedia, http://en.wikipedia.org/ wiki/Thomas_Robert_Malthus.

158 To measure savings rates, we used National Economic Accounts data, which is compiled by the Bureau of Economic Analysis. The relevant metric is "Personal Saving as a Percentage of Disposable Personal Income." This data can be found under that heading at http://www.bea.gov/search/index.cfm.

159 This data can be found at www.standardandpoors.com.

160 Our source for data on income concentration was a study conducted by Piketty and Saez entitled "Income Inequality in the United States, 1913–1998" and published in the *Quarterly Journal of Economics*. The study was updated through 2008. The

study used individual income tax return data to estimate the distribution of income in the United States (http://elsa.berkeley .edu/~saez/). We tracked the percentage of total income earned by the top 1 percent of earners.

161　The Conference Board's Consumer Confidence Index can be found at www.conference-board.org/data/consumerdata.cfm.

162　This data can be obtained (at a subscription charge) at http:// mailmonitor.synovate.com.

163　"Senior Loan Officer Opinion Survey on Bank Lending Practices," The Federal Reserve Board, www.federalreserve.gov/ boarddocs/SnLoanSurvey.

164　"Consumer Credit Outstanding," The Federal Reserve Board, www.federalreserve.gov/releases/g19/hist/cc_hist_sa.txt.

165　BusinessDictionary.com, www.businessdictionary.com/definition/ personal-savings-rate.html.

166　Daryl G. Jones, "Personal Savings Rate: Worse than We Thought," *Fortune,* CNNMoney.com, http://money.cnn .com/2010/06/30/news/economy/personal_savings_decline .fortune/index.htm.

167　Standard & Poor's Bureau of Economic Analysis

168　Thomas Piketty and Emmanuel Saez, "Income Inequality in the United States, 1913–1998," *Quarterly Journal of Economics,* 118(1), 2003. Updated to 2008.

169　Ibid.

170　Ibid.

171　Ibid.

172　Ibid.

173　"Consumer Confidence," Wikipedia, http://en.wikipedia.org/ wiki/Consumer_confidence.

174　Standard & Poor's Conference Board.

175　The regression equation is the following:
S&P 500 Estimate = -777.5 + (2.09) * (Consumer Confidence) + (9,193.4) * (Income Concentration) – (3,805.1) * (Savings

Rate). As an example, let's use the twenty-year quarterly averages for each of the variables. The twenty-year average for Consumer Confidence was 94.3; the average for Income Concentration was 18.3 percent; and the average for Savings Rate was 4.4 percent. If we plug these values into the regression equation, our estimate for the S&P 500 would be 931—well below today's level of about 1,150.

176　Standard & Poor's proprietary regression analysis uses data from the Bureau of Economic Analysis, Piketty & Saez, and the Conference Board.

INDEX

absolute certainty, 152–54

acceptance, as Arrogance Cycle stage, 28, 31

Access International, 75, 77–78

accounting practices, 133–36

Acey-Deucey studies, 35–37

addiction, 34–35

Adjustable Rate Mortgages, 50

advertising, 2, 13–14, 113–14, 148

Afghanistan war, 21–22

AIG (American International Group), 48, 89–94

Aislabie, John, 107

Ali, Muhammad, 56

Allen, Frederick Lewis, 109–10

American Dream, 9–12

American International Group (AIG), 48

Arrogance Cycles, overview. *See also* bubbles
  characteristics and challenges of, 95–100
  in history, examples of, 100–117, 185–86
  stages of, 28–31

Arthur Andersen, 85, 133–35

asset prices, 172–73

Atlas Shrugged (Rand), 32–33

auditors, 134

average, 1–2

Babson, Roger, 112

Baby Boomer generation, 8–10, 12–14

bailouts, 92, 103

Bankers Trust, 130–31

banking deregulation, 130–33

Bank of America, 46

Bank of New York, 61

Barnette, Jeff, 193

Bear Stearns, 71, 80–81

belonging, 52, 54, 73–75, 158–60, 191–92

Bernanke, Ben S., 68–69

Big Short, The (Lewis), 193

Black Tuesday, 109–10

Bliley, Thomas J., Jr., 124

Blunt, John, 105–6

bonuses, 72–73

brain function, 33–35

Breiter, Hans, 34

bubbles
  in American history, 109–15
  behavior characteristics of, 183–85
  in European history, 99–105
  examples of, 105–9
  stock market indicators of, 171–82
  truth and, 190–91

Buechner, Frederick, 192